Igniting Excellence: Challenges of a First-Year Fire Chief

Eric J. Neal

Published by Eric J. Neal, 2024.

While every precaution has been taken in the preparation of this book, the publisher assumes no responsibility for errors or omissions, or for damages resulting from the use of the information contained herein.

IGNITING EXCELLENCE: CHALLENGES OF A FIRST-YEAR FIRE CHIEF

First edition. December 6, 2024.

Copyright © 2024 Eric J. Neal.

ISBN: 979-8230003526

Written by Eric J. Neal.

Table of Contents

Dedication

To the brave men and women of the fire service who dedicate their lives to protecting others. To my mentors, colleagues, and family who inspired and supported me throughout my journey. And to those stepping into leadership—may this book guide and encourage you to ignite excellence in all you do.

Written by Fire Chief Eric J. Neal, *Igniting Excellence* is a candid account of his first year as a fire chief. Neal shares personal stories of navigating leadership challenges, building trust, and making critical decisions. This insightful guide offers inspiration and practical lessons for aspiring and current leaders in fire service.

Chapter 1: Overcoming Personal Challenges

A Fire Chief's Journey

Overcoming personal challenges is an intrinsic part of life's journey, and this chapter delves into Eric J. Neal's narrative, illustrating how determination and resilience can reshape one's path. The decision to leave Memphis for Arlington wasn't merely a change of scenery for Eric; it marked the start of a new pursuit, prioritizing family safety and career prospects amid daunting circumstances. His commitment to a better life brought him face-to-face with substantial sacrifices, including leaving behind familiar surroundings and a secure position. Yet, these hurdles were not deterrents but rather steppingstones fueling his resolve to achieve both personal stability and professional growth.

The chapter explores Eric's dual existence, where balancing obligations in two cities tested his fortitude. His story unfolds through the lens of significant transitions—starting over in Arlington's competitive job market while furthering education to strengthen his career prospects. Readers will discover the depth of Eric's challenges as he navigates strenuous commutes and taxing schedules, juxtaposed with intense personal struggles like enduring toxic relationships and facing legal battles. Through each segment of his journey in Arlington, we observe how Eric's choices were guided by a deliberate focus on safety, family well-being, and career aspirations, exemplifying perseverance under pressure.

The Memphis Years and Moving Forward

The decision to relocate from Memphis to Arlington was a turning point in Eric J. Neal's life, marked by a strong desire to prioritize family safety and seek better career opportunities. Living in a neighborhood plagued by crime meant constant worry for his family's well-being, which often overshadowed even his deepest career ambitions. With crime rates soaring and the streets becoming more precarious day by day, the urgency to find a more stable environment grew stronger. His career as an officer in Memphis provided him with valuable experience, but the city's conditions made it challenging to balance professional duties with personal responsibilities. Thus, the search for a safer haven led him to Arlington, a place where he envisioned both a secure home life and prospects that aligned with his aspirations.

Transitioning to a new city comes with its own set of challenges, and for Eric, this move tested his resolve in unprecedented ways. He was faced with the daunting task of maintaining his professional commitments in Memphis while exploring opportunities in Arlington. This duality put immense physical and emotional stress on him, as he struggled to juggle obligations in two places without letting either suffer. The daily routine became a grueling schedule of long commutes and strenuous work hours, leaving little room for rest or personal time. Despite the exhaustion, Eric remained committed to securing a brighter future for his family, determined not to let immediate hardships cloud his long-term vision.

Rebuilding his career from the ground up in Arlington meant leaving behind the established status and professional recognition he had earned over years of dedicated service in Memphis. Starting anew was no small feat, particularly when it involved letting go of the security and respect that came with his former position. This sacrifice was compounded by the reality of entering a competitive job market where his past achievements only held so much weight. Eric had to demonstrate resilience and adaptability, proving himself once again to potential employers who were unfamiliar with his track record. It was a humbling journey, one that reminded him of the value of perseverance and the importance of staying true to his goals despite the sacrifices required.

One of the most taxing aspects of this phase was enduring the long commutes between Memphis and Arlington. These were not just physically demanding; they also posed a significant mental strain, as Eric grappled with uncertainty about securing a stable job in Arlington. Each trip symbolized his unwavering commitment to his family's welfare, a constant test of his dedication to their happiness and security. The fear of job insecurity loomed large, yet it fueled his determination rather than dampening his spirit. Eric's resolve was unyielding, driven by the understanding that every mile traveled brought him closer to achieving the stability he sought for those he cared about most.

Throughout this tumultuous period, Eric found that his decisions were deeply influenced by a triad of critical factors: safety, family welfare, and career aspirations. The interplay between these elements guided his choices, shaping the path he would take to navigate his personal and professional life. In prioritizing safety, he ensured that his family could thrive in a nurturing environment free from the threats they faced in Memphis. Balancing family needs with career growth required compromise and forethought, as he weighed the implications of each step within the broader picture of their future. While the journey was fraught with obstacles, each challenge reaffirmed the necessity of his decisions, reinforcing the belief that his efforts would eventually bear fruit.

Starting Over and Educational Pursuits

Eric J. Neal's path to becoming Fire Chief is a remarkable testament to the power of reinvention through resilience and education. At the age of 42, when many might see their career paths as well-defined, Eric made the bold decision to transition from an experienced officer in Memphis to a new recruit in Arlington. This move wasn't just about changing locations; it was about proving himself all over again. Despite the challenges that come with such a significant change later in life, Eric's dedication to demonstrating his capabilities anew fueled his journey.

In Arlington, where he essentially started from scratch, Eric embraced the opportunity to show what decades of experience had afforded him. The courage to step into a role traditionally filled by younger recruits speaks volumes about his confidence and commitment. But it wasn't just about proving himself capable; it was about setting a foundation for continuous growth and learning.

To move beyond traditional hierarchies and constraints that could limit his potential, Eric strategically opted to further his education. He pursued a bachelor's degree in emergency management, followed by a master's in public administration. This educational journey was not only a personal achievement but also a critical tool in advancing his career. It allowed him to bypass conventional obstacles often faced in hierarchical professions, especially those encountered by individuals trying to climb ranks anew in midlife. Education empowered Eric, providing him with knowledge and credentials that stood out amidst competitive environments, ultimately contributing significantly to his ability to secure roles that matched his aspirations.

Yet, Eric's professional journey was paralleled by profound personal challenges. Reaching a breaking point in his personal life, he faced tough decisions. Realizing the toll of maintaining toxic relationships, he chose self-respect above all, opting for divorce. This decision was pivotal, marking a new beginning; it symbolized his commitment to personal happiness and clarity. The importance of choosing one's well-being, even at great personal cost, cannot be overstated, and Eric's decision set a precedent for taking decisive action when confronted with adverse circumstances.

As if this were not enough, Eric's integrity came under fire when he faced legal battles and false accusations. These challenges threatened his professional standing and could have easily derailed his career. However, Eric remained steadfast, holding on to his principles and pushing back against these formidable odds. His unwavering sense of integrity, coupled with his qualifications, helped him navigate through these turbulent times. Rather than allowing the situation to defeat him, Eric saw these challenges as opportunities to reinforce his character and determination.

Despite these hurdles, his relentless spirit and tangible accomplishments in the field secured him a leadership role in Pecos. Overcoming adversity once again underscored Eric's exceptional ability to rise above difficulties and stand firm in his professional arena. It's a journey that illustrates not just survival but thriving in face of adversity—a journey where resilience and education became the cornerstones of his ascent to leadership.

For those who find themselves facing seemingly insurmountable challenges, Eric's journey serves as both an inspiration and a blueprint. Reinventing oneself is not solely about adapting to immediate situations; it involves a strategic and thoughtful approach that harnesses education and personal growth. As we observe Eric's story, it's clear that rising above life's persistently difficult tests requires more than just perseverance—it calls for an embrace of continuous learning and an unyielding belief in one's own values.

Guidelines gleaned from Eric's approach highlight crucial steps for those aiming for similar transformations. By investing in education that aligns with one's career goals, individuals can unlock doors previously thought closed. Moreover, understanding the necessity of personal well-being and prioritizing it even in challenging times ensures a stronger foundation from which to tackle professional ambitions. Learning from setbacks, and more importantly, deriving strength from them, is vital transforming each challenge into a stepping stone rather than a stumbling block.

6

Summary and Reflections

Eric J. Neal's journey to becoming Fire Chief illustrates a profound narrative of resilience and determination in both his personal and professional spheres. Moving from Memphis, Eric faced the daunting task of rebuilding a career and life amidst numerous challenges. His dedication to family safety and professional growth drove him through periods of uncertainty and hardship. Each obstacle met with unyielding resolve highlighted his commitment to ensuring a brighter future for his loved ones. This journey reveals the immense strength needed to balance familial responsibilities while pursuing one's ambitions, serving as an inspiration to those encountering similar circumstances.

The path Eric took underscores the powerful impact of continuous learning and self-reinvention. By embracing education, he strategically positioned himself to overcome traditional barriers and secure his desired roles. Simultaneously, Eric's personal struggles, including difficult decisions like ending toxic relationships, reflect the necessity of prioritizing well-being amid adversity. Through these experiences, he exemplified how integrity and resilience can shape and define one's professional trajectory. Eric's story is not just about enduring but thriving despite challenges—a testament to the transformative power of perseverance and education that inspires individuals facing their battles.

Chapter 2: A Fiery Beginning

The First Day as Fire Chief

Assuming the responsibilities of a Fire Chief presents a unique blend of pressures and opportunities, encapsulating a crucial shift in leadership dynamics. On his first day as the newly appointed Fire Chief of Balch Springs, Neal faced both anticipation and uncertainty. The significance of this role was not lost on him; it demanded immediate acclimatization to new environments and protocols. Transitioning from firefighter to a leader required more than just operational expertise; it necessitated a profound understanding of interpersonal dynamics and strategic foresight. This initial day marked a pivotal moment where Neal's vision for the department began to take form amidst the backdrop of expectations set by both his predecessors and peers.

In this chapter, the narrative unfolds revealing Neal's approach to navigating these inaugural challenges while emphasizing the importance of building trust within his team. It explores his efforts to foster an inclusive culture that values diverse perspectives and experiences. Neal's commitment to enhancing departmental efficiency through continuous training and readiness is highlighted along with his personal leadership philosophy shaped by resilience and past adversities. As the section progresses, readers gain insight into how Neal strategically balances tradition with innovation, maintaining a reverence for established practices while simultaneously embracing modernization. This dual focus not only aims to solidify the fire department's identity but also prepares it for future exigencies. Ultimately, the chapter delves into Neal's reflective practices which guide his ongoing journey of principled leadership, highlighting his resolve to cultivate a legacy defined by unity and excellence.

Stepping into the Shoes

Chief Neal's journey to becoming the Fire Chief of Balch Springs is a testament to resilience and dedication. His career began in Memphis, a city known for its robust firefighting community. It was here that he donned his first uniform, fueled by a desire to make a difference. The camaraderie among his fellow firefighters in Memphis played a pivotal role in his development. They shared stories, techniques, and the occasional humorous tale from their shifts, building a strong foundation of mutual support and learning. These experiences were crucial as they shaped his understanding of teamwork and leadership.

In Memphis, Neal quickly proved himself adept at managing high-pressure situations, forging bonds with both rookie and veteran firefighters. This environment taught Neal valuable lessons in trust and cooperation, often unspoken yet deeply ingrained through intense collaborative efforts during emergencies. As he climbed the ranks, these foundational experiences became critical assets that would guide him in more senior roles.

Transitioning from an urban landscape to suburban challenges presented a whole new set of obstacles for Neal when he moved from Arlington to Balch Springs. In Arlington, the demands were relentless, with skyscrapers and busy streets dictating a fast-paced response. The skills honed there were different; it required agility, quick decision-making, and constant adaptation to complex infrastructure. However, Balch Springs' comparatively quieter suburban setting brought a different rhythm. Here, the focus shifted from skyscrapers to small communities, from bustling traffic to residential safety, requiring a broader perspective on resource management and preparation for diverse scenarios.

While both environments needed a careful balance of reactive and proactive strategies, Neal recognized that a one-size-fits-all approach wouldn't suffice. Each call in Balch Springs offered unique challenges—from wildfires affecting suburban homes to accidents on less congested roads—requiring recalibrated responses compared to those in Arlington. This shift demanded Neal harness both his experience and creativity, tailoring his strategies to fit this new context.

As Neal settled into his role, building trust within the existing firehouse emerged as a priority. The crew in Balch Springs came from a variety of backgrounds, each bringing their own perspectives and experiences to the table. Bridging these gaps was essential. Neal invested time in understanding each team member individually, emphasizing open communication and fostering inclusion. He made it clear that each voice mattered, eliciting ideas and feedback to build a cohesive unit.

Guidelines for building trust became integral: establishing transparent communication channels, engaging in regular team-building activities, and upholding mutual respect regardless of rank or tenure. By focusing on these principles, Neal was able to create a harmonious work environment despite initial skepticism, earning respect through consistent dedication to unity and integrity.

Furthermore, honoring the traditions of Balch Springs while embracing modern challenges was a balancing act Neal approached with sensitivity and foresight. The traditions held deep significance, embodying the spirit and history of the community. Yet, to be effective, integrating contemporary methodologies and technology was indispensable. This required strategic vision: respecting longstanding values while aligning them with innovative practices that could enhance operational effectiveness.

Neal initiated programs that celebrated the department's past achievements—reminding the team of their roots—while concurrently investing in training sessions focused on new-age firefighting techniques and equipment. This dual approach not only ensured compatibility between tradition and innovation but also signaled to the team that progress, and preservation could coexist. By doing so,

Neal strengthened the department's identity, fostering pride and enthusiasm for both its heritage and its future trajectory.

Throughout this transformation, Neal remained mindful of the delicate interplay between leading and listening. He recognized that true leadership wasn't about commanding from above but uplifting from within. By valuing each firefighter's input and creating a culture where questions and suggestions were welcomed, he empowered his team to excel collectively. This evolved the firehouse into not just a place of work but a haven of mutual growth and shared mission.

The First Briefing and Evening Reflection

Stepping into his role as Fire Chief, Neal's first day was marked with a myriad of emotions and expectations. His primary objective during the initial staff briefing was to convey a vision that resonated with openness and transparency. It was crucial for him to cultivate an environment where communication flowed freely, fostering collaboration among his team members. At that gathering, he articulated his commitment to these principles, emphasizing their importance in achieving collective success.

Open dialogue and adaptability were themes he returned to throughout the meeting. Chief Neal understood that the unpredictable nature of firefighting required a team adept at adjusting to rapidly changing situations. By encouraging his staff to voice their opinions and share experiences, Neal sought to empower them to take initiative. He believed that a collaborative culture would not only enhance decision-making but also build trust and unity within the department.

In addressing departmental efficiency, Neal highlighted the significance of continuous training and equipment readiness. He knew that maintaining peak performance was essential for the safety of both his team and the community they served. Stressing this point, he shared plans for frequent drills and training sessions, designed to keep skills sharp and to swiftly integrate new techniques and technologies. Equipment checks would become routine, ensuring everything functioned optimally preparing the team for any eventuality.

Personal tragedy had shaped Neal's leadership style, infusing it with resilience and dedication. This personal history was a lens through which he viewed his responsibilities, instilling in him a determination to lead by example. While he didn't delve deep into personal stories with his team on that first day, the gravity of these experiences was subtly felt in his demeanor. His steadfastness inspired those around him, encouraging them to approach challenges with equal tenacity.

Unity through diversity was another cornerstone Neal emphasized, aiming to foster inclusivity and respect. In the diverse landscape of the fire department, creating an environment where every individual felt valued was paramount. Neal proposed initiatives to celebrate varied cultural backgrounds and perspectives, understanding that such diversity strengthened their collective ability to innovate and problem-solve. By championing different viewpoints, he hoped to break down barriers and build bridges within the team.

With the briefing concluded and the day's challenges navigated, Neal took a moment to reflect on his achievements and areas of growth. Walking through the firehouse, he noted the camaraderie among his team—a direct result of the inclusive atmosphere he had nurtured. However, he was also mindful of the tasks still ahead: refining strategies, reinforcing training protocols, and continually nurturing the sense of unity he valued.

Neal knew that the path forward would demand more than just perseverance; it would require unwavering dedication to principles he held dear. He often pondered over his experiences, drawing lessons from both triumphs and setbacks, shaping him into a leader who understood the balance between firmness and empathy.

As he settled into his new office, Neal considered how best to gear up for future challenges. Flexibility in problem-solving and the capacity to pivot strategies swiftly were crucial components he intended to embed deeply within the team's ethos. He began drafting guidelines to support this, crafting policies that promoted agility without compromising the department's core values or operational integrity.

His reflections extended to the broader implications of leadership, contemplating how his journey could inspire others. Though he recognized the gravity of his position, Neal appreciated the opportunity to mold the department into a beacon of excellence. He saw potential in each interaction, viewing challenges not as impediments but as catalysts for meaningful change.

Above all, Neal aspired to leave a legacy defined by more than just firefighting prowess. He envisioned a department celebrated for its compassion and dedication to service, one that transcended differences in pursuit of a common goal. As he penned his thoughts, the draft emerged not merely as a manual for operations but a testament to the values he championed: integrity, unity, and relentless pursuit of excellence.

Final Insights

Chief Neal's first day as Fire Chief in Balch Springs showcased his dedication to fostering an inclusive and cooperative environment. He emphasized the importance of open dialogue, adaptability, and continuous training to ensure his team was prepared for any situation. These principles, rooted in Neal's personal experiences and leadership style, were critical as he worked to build trust within his diverse team. By valuing each firefighter's input and cultural background, Neal aimed to create a harmonious atmosphere where innovation and problem-solving thrived.

Reflecting on his initial achievements, Neal recognized the journey ahead, which required both perseverance and adaptability. His approach to leadership was shaped by understanding the balance between firmness and empathy, crucial for overcoming the unique challenges in Balch Springs. As he navigated his new role, Neal envisioned molding the department into a beacon of excellence and compassion, transcending differences in pursuit of common goals. His legacy would be defined not only by operational success but also by the unity and integrity he cultivated within his team.

Chapter 3: Setting the Stage

Preparing for Year One

Preparing for the first year in a leadership role involves meticulous planning and strategic foresight. For Chief Eric J. Neal, assuming command of the Balch Springs Fire Department required laying a robust foundation upon which future success could be built. His approach was not about immediate changes but about establishing a framework that would sustain operational excellence and foster an environment conducive to growth. This chapter explores how strategic planning becomes the cornerstone for organizational stability, particularly in a critical public service sector like fire safety. The ability to lead effectively during challenging times requires both visionary thinking and grounded action, elements that define Chief Neal's tenure.

Setting the stage for his ambitious plans, Chief Neal initiated a thorough examination of the department's capabilities and potential areas for development. Readers will delve into the specifics of his administrative strategy, including how assessing current strengths and weaknesses provided the insights necessary for guiding the department forward. The chapter also sheds light on Chief Neal's emphasis on building strong internal relationships through clear communication and accountability. Furthermore, it discusses his efforts to engage with the community and local stakeholders, illustrating his commitment to collaborative progress. By understanding these foundational aspects, one gains insight into the complexities faced by Chief Neal and the innovative approaches he adopted to navigate them successfully.

Mastering Administrative and Strategic Planning

Chief Eric J. Neal's first year at the helm of the Balch Springs Fire Department was all about setting a solid foundation for the organization's future success. In the process, he aimed to establish a clear administrative and strategic framework that would guide the department in overcoming challenges and achieving its objectives.

To begin with, Chief Neal conducted a comprehensive assessment of the department's current strengths and weaknesses. This involved an in-depth review of existing policies, procedures, and overall readiness to respond to emergencies. By examining these fundamental aspects, Chief Neal could identify where the department excelled and where there were gaps in the system. This approach wasn't just about pointing out deficiencies; it was also a chance to celebrate what the team was doing well. For instance, successful policy implementations from the past served as benchmarks for creating effective future strategies.

After gathering this information, Chief Neal set about developing a strategic roadmap. This plan was not merely a document to be filed away but served as a guiding vision to align departmental activities with key priorities and objectives. The roadmap emphasized enhancing operational efficiency and service delivery, which are critical components in any emergency response organization. Part of this initiative included streamlining communication channels and ensuring that all team members understood their roles and responsibilities. Moreover, by setting clear goals, the department could track progress and adjust tactics as needed, maintaining flexibility while remaining focused on long-term objectives.

In fostering an environment of accountability, Chief Neal prioritized open, clear communication within the department. He understood that for any organization to thrive, every team member must feel connected and responsible for their role in its success. Encouraging teamwork was pivotal; it not only built camaraderie among firefighters but also ensured that the department functioned as a cohesive unit during emergencies. Strategies to promote accountability included regular meetings where firefighters could share concerns and successes, providing a platform for transparency and mutual support.

Transparency and collaboration were equally important in developing strong internal relationships. Chief Neal highlighted the necessity of open dialogues and active listening as tools to motivate staff and optimize resources. When team members felt heard and valued, they were more likely to contribute positively towards collective goals. Additionally, by creating avenues for feedback and discussion, Chief Neal paved the way for continuous improvement and innovation within the department. Collaborative efforts extended beyond internal operations to involve local stakeholders, ensuring alignment with community expectations and leveraging external resources efficiently.

A significant part of building this framework involved fostering a culture of mutual trust and respect. This was achieved through initiatives that encouraged personal growth and professional development. Training sessions, workshops, and seminars became integral parts of the fire department's routine, equipping staff with the necessary skills and knowledge to excel in their duties. These educational initiatives were designed not only to advance individual capabilities but also to strengthen the team's overall competence and confidence.

Additionally, Chief Neal recognized the power of leading by example. His commitment to the department's mission and his accessibility to both officers and rookies alike demonstrated his dedication to the cause. By being present and actively participating in daily activities, Chief Neal reinforced the values of integrity and dedication, further inspiring his team to strive towards excellence.

In essence, Chief Neal's strategic planning was holistic, considering not only the operational aspects of the fire department but also the human elements that drive its success. By laying down a strong administrative and strategic framework, he positioned the Balch Springs Fire Department for future achievements. Through careful assessment, deliberate planning, and fostering a culture of accountability and transparency, Chief Neal established a legacy of resilience and resourcefulness that the department could build upon in the years to come.

Building Relationships and Facing Challenges

Building trust and unity within the department, while navigating external challenges, is a critical task that Chief Eric J. Neal faced in his first year leading the Balch Springs Fire Department. Recognizing the importance of stakeholder relationships was fundamental to this goal. Engaging with local officials, neighboring departments, and the community became a cornerstone of his approach. By fostering these connections, Chief Neal ensured that the fire department was not only seen as an essential emergency service but as a collaborative partner within the community.

One significant step he took was actively participating in local events, allowing community members to interact with their firefighters on a personal level. This involvement extended beyond ceremonial appearances. The chief organized joint training exercises with nearby fire departments, creating opportunities for shared learning and mutual support. Such initiatives helped build a network of partnerships that enhanced operational efficiency and public perception.

Navigating the City Council's divided opinion on his leadership vision proved to be a pivotal challenge. Chief Neal approached this by engaging council members individually, presenting his plans and listening to their concerns. Through strategic alliances, he demonstrated how his vision aligned with the city's broader goals. For instance, by highlighting enhancements in response times and improved safety protocols, he appealed to both efficiency-focused and safety-conscious council members.

Guidelines become crucial here: Chief Neal engaged in open dialogue, holding town hall meetings where community members and council members could voice their opinions and concerns. He provided clear, evidence-based responses to council inquiries, reinforcing trust through transparency. Establishing a feedback loop allowed him to adapt his strategies according to the evolving political landscape, thereby gaining gradual council support.

Within the department, addressing the mixed emotions among firefighters required promoting open dialogue and empathy. The transition in leadership naturally brought uncertainty. Some firefighters were apprehensive about changes, fearing disruptions to long-standing traditions. Chief Neal prioritized open communication, encouraging feedback through regular team meetings and one-on-one sessions. These conversations were instrumental in understanding the concerns and aspirations of his team.

By implementing empathy-driven practices, such as active listening and validating the feelings of his team members, Chief Neal fostered a supportive environment. He emphasized the significance of every firefighter's contribution, celebrating small victories to boost morale and reinforce a sense of belonging. Over time, these efforts cultivated a culture of trust and unity, reducing resistance to change and enhancing overall department cohesion.

Establishing guidelines for internal communication was vital in nurturing this environment. Ensuring that all voices were heard, Chief Neal introduced structured channels for suggestions and grievances. An anonymous feedback system was implemented to encourage candidness without fear of repercussion. This empowered firefighters to express their true feelings, leading to constructive discussions and collective problem-solving.

Balancing personal challenges with professional dedication further demonstrated Chief Neal's resilience. Leading a fire department requires unwavering commitment, yet personal adversities often demand attention. During his tenure, Chief Neal faced several such challenges, which he navigated without compromising his professional responsibilities. His ability to remain focused under pressure became a testament to his leadership qualities, inspiring those around him.

Chief Neal shared his experiences openly with his team, using them as teaching moments. By being vulnerable about his struggles, he fostered a culture where it was acceptable to seek help and prioritize mental well-being. This approach underscored the message that personal challenges do not detract from one's professional capabilities but can instead strengthen resolve and empathy toward others facing similar battles.

Concluding Thoughts

Chief Eric J. Neal's first year at the Balch Springs Fire Department was marked by deliberate efforts in strategic planning and community engagement. Throughout this period, he laid a robust foundation for the department, emphasizing clear communication, operational efficiency, and strong internal relationships. By conducting a thorough assessment, he identified both strengths and areas for improvement, setting the stage for future success. His approach was not just about policy adjustments but instilled a culture of accountability and participation among his team. The chapter highlights how Chief Neal's inclusive leadership style unified the department, enabling it to tackle challenges effectively while maintaining high morale.

Additionally, Chief Neal faced the intricate task of building trust both within the department and with external stakeholders. By actively engaging with local officials, communities, and neighboring departments, he fostered meaningful connections that positioned the fire department as a vital community ally. Navigating the City Council's diverse perspectives required careful dialogue and transparency, showcasing how his strategic vision aligned with the city's goals. With empathy and open communication, he managed internal transitions smoothly, ensuring every firefighter felt valued and heard. This chapter serves as a testament to Chief Neal's resilience and dedication, which paved the way for enduring improvements and set a significant precedent for continued excellence in emergency response services.

Chapter 4: The Fire Service Landscape

Challenges and Expectations

Navigating the fire service landscape presents a unique set of challenges that demand foresight and adaptability. As Chief Eric J. Neal steps into this evolving environment, his leadership is tested by the need to address the complexities inherent in suburban firefighting. In Balch Springs, where diverse residential areas coexist alongside industrial zones, the stakes are high. The demographic and structural variations of the community require bespoke solutions and innovative practices. Under Chief Neal's command, the fire department is revamping its strategies to meet these demands head-on, ensuring readiness for any scenario.

In this chapter, readers will delve into the meticulous efforts undertaken by Chief Neal as he leads the charge against various operational challenges. The text will explore how he adapts training programs to incorporate essential firefighting skills along with specialized techniques such as hazardous material handling and urban search and rescue operations. It will also shed light on his strategic partnerships with neighboring departments aimed at fostering collaboration and conducting joint exercises. Furthermore, attention will be given to the significant investments in state-of-the-art equipment needed to enhance response efficiency and safety. This exploration will reveal the comprehensive strategies employed to balance resource allocation while maintaining high standards of service amidst budgetary constraints. By examining Chief Neal's initiatives, readers gain insight into the intricacies of managing a modern fire department and the crucial role of leadership in navigating community expectations and operational necessities.

Navigating Shifting Dynamics and Resource Allocation

Chief Eric J. Neal finds himself at the helm of a fire department facing unprecedented challenges and expectations in Balch Springs. The dynamic nature of suburban firefighting requires an innovative approach to training and equipment, tailored to the specific needs of this community. Chief Neal recognizes that the demographic and structural makeup of Balch Springs demands unique adaptations. Residential areas are interspersed with industrial zones, creating diverse firefighting scenarios that require specialized training modules for his team.

Adapting training involves not just fire suppression skills but also proficiency in handling hazardous materials and urban search and rescue operations. In response, Chief Neal has implemented a series of targeted drills and simulations, ensuring that every firefighter is prepared for the multifaceted threats they might face. He has fostered partnerships with neighboring departments to conduct joint exercises, teaching firefighters how to collaborate effectively under pressure. This comprehensive approach not only boosts skill but also morale, as firefighters gain confidence through hands-on experience in realistic settings.

Equipment adaptation is another critical focus area. The rapid development in Balch Springs means continuous updates in technology and gear are needed to ensure optimal response capabilities. Chief Neal oversees the acquisition of multi-functional tools that enhance efficiency, such as thermal imaging cameras to detect heat signatures in burning buildings or adaptable hoses suited for both residential and industrial fires. By prioritizing state-of-the-art gear, Chief Neal ensures his team can act swiftly and safely, minimizing damage and safeguarding lives.

Transitioning from Care Flite to Medical Jets was a bold move aimed at improving response times and access to specialized medical care. Chief Neal understood that minutes could mean the difference between life and death during emergencies. With Medical Jets, the capability to provide advanced pre-hospital care during transit became a game-changer. This transition required strategic planning and cooperation with local hospitals and aviation providers to seamlessly integrate new protocols. Training sessions were conducted for EMS personnel to familiarize them with onboard medical equipment, ensuring they could deliver critical interventions effectively.

One of the most pressing challenges was managing budgetary constraints while maintaining high standards of service. Establishing a robust budget plan within limited timeframes demanded meticulous attention to detail and a proactive approach. Chief Neal initiated a thorough audit of existing expenditures, identifying areas where costs could be reduced without compromising safety or performance. He advocated for a transparent budgeting process, involving input from various stakeholders to address community priorities and operational necessities.

Guidelines were established to prioritize spending on essential services and capital improvements. This involved making tough decisions about deferring non-critical expenses to allocate funds toward indispensable resources. For example, upgrading communication systems within the department took precedence over aesthetic refurbishments, as reliable communications are vital during crises. Additionally, Chief Neal pursued grant opportunities and collaborative funding efforts with government agencies to supplement the financial shortfalls experienced by many fire departments.

Investing in essential services and cutting-edge technology is vital for maintaining professionalism and readiness. Beyond basic firefighting equipment, Chief Neal recognized the importance of investing in the well-being of his team. Adequate protective gear, mental health support programs, and continuing education opportunities were prioritized, reflecting his commitment to their overall welfare. The introduction of wellness programs and peer support networks illustrates his dedication to fostering a resilient and capable workforce.

Navigating these complex issues requires clear strategies and strong leadership to balance current demands with future preparedness. Chief Neal's stewardship is marked by an unwavering dedication to serving the Balch Springs community while ensuring that his department remains agile and responsive in a rapidly changing environment. He embodies the qualities of an adaptive leader, constantly evaluating and refining approaches to better meet the needs of those he serves.

Strengthening Workforce and Community Engagement

In recent years, the fire service has faced a multitude of challenges, compelling leaders like Chief Eric J. Neal to adapt and innovate to meet both internal demands and community expectations. One pivotal area demanding attention is recruitment and retention within fire departments. As the demands of the role evolve, so too must the strategies for attracting and retaining dedicated professionals who embody the values and mission of the department.

Recruitment initiatives are crucial in navigating the complexities of modern firefighting. Attracting qualified individuals who not only possess the necessary skills but also align with departmental values requires a strategic approach. This begins with crafting appealing job descriptions and using targeted marketing campaigns to reach diverse audiences. Potential recruits need to see themselves as integral parts of a team committed to excellence and community service. Innovative recruitment efforts might include participating in career fairs, conducting outreach at local schools, and offering internships or volunteer opportunities that provide hands-on experience in firefighting roles.

Once recruited, retaining these talented professionals poses another challenge. Chief Neal understands that developing robust retention programs is essential for maintaining a competent and motivated workforce. Competitive compensation packages play a significant role in retention, ensuring that firefighters feel valued and adequately rewarded for their dedication and hard work. Beyond monetary incentives, growth opportunities within the department can significantly boost morale and job satisfaction. Providing avenues for professional development, such as specialized training programs, leadership workshops, and pathways to promotion, empowers individuals to envision long-term careers within the organization.

Community engagement is another critical component of Chief Neal's strategy to enhance the fire department's relationship with the public it serves. Successful engagement initiatives go beyond standard practices, integrating workshops, educational programs, and safety awareness campaigns tailored to address the specific needs and interests of the community. Workshops might cover essential topics like fire prevention, home safety checks, and emergency preparedness, appealing to diverse age groups and demographics. Educational initiatives can introduce young people to fire safety concepts in engaging ways, building a foundation of awareness from an early age.

Actively fostering trust and relationships within the community is a priority under Chief Neal's leadership. By addressing community needs and expectations proactively, the department strengthens its bond with residents. Listening sessions, where community members express concerns and provide feedback, allow for open dialogue. Firefighters participating in local events or volunteering for community services signifies their investment in the neighborhoods they serve, reinforcing the perception of firefighters as integral parts of the community fabric.

Chief Neal recognizes that effective communication forms the backbone of successful community outreach and engagement. Regular newsletters, social media updates, and partnerships with local media outlets ensure that the community remains informed and engaged with the fire department's initiatives and accomplishments. These communication channels also serve to highlight the department's transparency and accountability, further solidifying community trust.

Understanding the importance of diversity and inclusion, Chief Neal implements guidelines to create a welcoming environment for all. Recruitment efforts focus on attracting candidates from varied backgrounds, emphasizing the value of diverse perspectives in enhancing team dynamics and decision-making processes. Retention strategies include mentoring programs and affinity groups, promoting inclusivity and providing support networks for minority colleagues.

Moreover, continuous community engagement cannot be successfully sustained without adequate funding and resources. It becomes imperative for fire departments to advocate for budget allocations that support these initiatives. Demonstrating the positive impact of engagement programs—such as decreased response times, improved public safety metrics, and heightened community satisfaction—provides compelling evidence for securing necessary resources.

Summary and Reflections

Chief Eric J. Neal's leadership in navigating the evolving landscape of fire service demonstrates a commitment to innovation and community-oriented solutions. The chapter highlights how Chief Neal has addressed the unique challenges faced by Balch Springs through focused training, equipment adaptation, and strategic resource allocation. By fostering collaborations with neighboring departments and implementing rigorous training simulations, he has effectively equipped his team to handle diverse firefighting scenarios. His foresight in transitioning to Medical Jets illustrates a proactive approach to enhancing emergency response times and improving medical care access, even within stringent budget constraints. Through meticulous financial planning and targeted spending, Chief Neal ensures that both operational efficiency and firefighter welfare are not compromised, underscoring his dedication to a resilient and prepared department.

Furthermore, Chief Neal places significant emphasis on workforce development and community engagement as integral elements of his strategy. Recognizing the dynamic nature of modern firefighting, he employs innovative recruitment efforts and robust retention programs to attract and maintain a dedicated team. Simultaneously, his initiatives extend beyond internal operations, focusing on building trust and strong relationships with the community. Through educational workshops, safety campaigns, and open dialogue sessions, Chief Neal addresses the specific needs of residents, fostering mutual respect and cooperation. His commitment to transparency and inclusivity reflects an understanding that effective communication and diversity strengthen the department's capabilities, ensuring it remains responsive and engaged with those it serves.

Chapter 5: Building Trust and Camaraderie in the Team

Team Trust

Building trust and camaraderie within a team is essential for any successful organization, especially one as vital as the fire department. The cohesive bond among firefighters not only boosts morale but also enhances operational effectiveness, crucial in times of crisis. This chapter delves into the different dimensions of teamwork within the fire department, elucidating how these aspects contribute to a unified front when tackling emergency situations. It explores the importance of strategic partnerships and regular meetings with key stakeholders, such as the City Manager, to ensure alignment with broader community objectives. From synchronizing resources to setting shared targets, these initiatives play a pivotal role in cultivating an environment where collaboration thrives.

As the chapter unfolds, readers will gain insight into various strategies employed by the fire department to foster unity both internally and with the broader community. It highlights collaborations with departments like Economic Development and local law enforcement, illustrating how these partnerships intertwine public safety with economic growth. The narrative emphasizes the significance of joint training exercises and community engagement through town hall meetings and disaster preparedness workshops. By adopting a transparent and inclusive approach, the department not only builds trust but also empowers community members to take an active role in their safety. Through real-world examples and practical guidelines, this chapter provides a comprehensive understanding of how camaraderie and trust are foundational to effective leadership and resilient communities.

Camaraderie Through Collaboration

Strategic partnerships play a crucial role in enhancing team unity and effectiveness within the fire department and throughout the broader community. Regular meetings with the City Manager are a key component of this strategy. These interactions ensure that the department's goals are aligned with the city's overarching objectives. This alignment fosters cooperation and a sense of shared purpose, as both the department and the city strive toward common targets. By syncing their efforts, they create a harmonious relationship where resources can be allocated more efficiently, projects can proceed smoothly, and mutual support becomes second nature.

The collaboration between the fire department and the Economic Development team further exemplifies the benefits of strategic partnerships. Through these collaborations, safety efforts are linked directly to economic growth initiatives, illustrating the mutual advantages each entity brings to the table. For instance, by ensuring public safety through effective response systems and proactive risk management, the fire department helps maintain an environment conducive to attracting new businesses and supporting local enterprises. This symbiotic relationship underscores how the safety and well-being of the community are foundational to its economic vitality and how economic prosperity can, in turn, provide additional resources for safety enhancements.

Joint training exercises with the police department highlight another layer of strategic partnership, showcasing the importance of inter-departmental trust. These training sessions are not just about honing technical skills but also about building a rapport between firefighters and law enforcement officers. The drills allow both teams to understand each other's operational methods and communication styles, which is critical during real emergency situations. When both teams act as cohesive units, it greatly improves their ability to coordinate responses effectively, thereby boosting the confidence of the community in their public safety agencies. As these relationships develop, the foundation of trust built upon familiarity and joint experiences paves the way for smoother operations and increased morale among personnel.

Viewing city leadership roles like positions on a football team offers an insightful analogy that further enhances understanding of strategic partnerships. Every leader, much like a player on a team, has a unique set of skills and perspectives that contribute to the overall success of the group. By recognizing the distinct roles and contributions of each member, leaders can cultivate an environment where everyone feels valued and accountable. This approach highlights the importance of diversity in thought and action, where different viewpoints come together to solve complex problems. It also emphasizes the necessity for clear communication and coordinated effort, much like in a well-executed game plan on the field. By fostering this type of collaborative spirit, the entire team functions more cohesively, leading to more innovative solutions and robust strategies.

Guidelines outlining how to build trust and camaraderie with the City Council can serve as a practical roadmap for developing these strategic partnerships. Establishing regular communication channels with council members is essential, as it opens pathways for dialogue and feedback, promoting transparency and accountability. Furthermore, engaging in joint projects or community initiatives with the council can strengthen these ties. Such collaborations could involve neighborhood safety programs or public outreach campaigns that align with both the council's and the department's goals. These endeavors not only nurture mutual respect and trust but also enhance the department's visibility and credibility within the community, solidifying its role as a proactive partner in local governance.

Trust in the Community

Transparency and inclusivity are foundational elements in building trust between a community and its local services, such as the fire department. One method of enhancing this relationship is through town hall meetings, which serve as an invaluable platform for open dialogue. During these gatherings, community members have the opportunity to voice their opinions, concerns, and feedback directly to those who lead local services. This form of engagement not only involves citizens in decision-making processes but also empowers them to feel like active participants in shaping policies that affect their lives. The regularity and sincerity of these meetings help reinforce the notion that every voice matters, fostering a deeper sense of collective responsibility and ownership within the community.

Open communication is another pillar of building trust. When a fire department openly discusses its challenges with the public—be it budget constraints, staffing issues, or operational hurdles—it strengthens community confidence and accountability. By keeping the dialogue transparent, departments can align their goals with community expectations, ensuring that both parties work together towards common objectives. For instance, by openly sharing challenges related to equipment upgrades or maintenance, the department may receive constructive suggestions or even volunteer assistance from the community. This transparency not only builds trust but also paves the way for collaborative problem-solving, where community members feel invested in the welfare of their local services.

Further reinforcing this trust is the commitment to diversity and inclusivity within the fire department itself. A department that mirrors the diverse demographic makeup of its community is more likely to foster a sense of belonging and trust among residents. Initiatives aimed at increasing diversity within the ranks not only provide equal opportunities for all but also ensure that the department better understands and represents the community it serves. Such representation is crucial in addressing the unique needs and concerns of different community segments, ultimately creating a more responsive and engaged service. Moreover, when residents see themselves reflected in local services, it cultivates a shared identity and mutual respect between the department and the community.

Disaster preparedness workshops represent yet another avenue through which community trust is fortified. By organizing and facilitating these workshops, fire departments equip residents with essential skills and knowledge needed to respond effectively in emergencies. These sessions, which cover topics ranging from basic first aid to emergency evacuation plans, empower individuals with the tools necessary to protect themselves and their families. Importantly, these workshops foster a proactive approach to shared resilience, encouraging communities to take an active role in their safety and well-being. As residents become more informed and prepared, their confidence in local services grows, knowing that their fire department is committed to safeguarding the community and ensuring its readiness in times of crisis.

Providing guidelines on developing and participating in a Community Emergency Response Team (CERT) can further deepen this connection. CERT programs offer volunteers specialized training to support first responders during emergencies. Participation in such teams allows community members to contribute meaningfully while gaining valuable skills. The presence of a CERT team within a community not only enhances the coordination and effectiveness of emergency response efforts but also solidifies the bond between residents and their local services, as they collaborate in real-time scenarios.

Bringing It All Together

This chapter delved into the importance of fostering strong relationships and trust within the fire department and with the broader community. Through strategic partnerships, such as those with city leaders and other municipal departments, the fire department can align its goals with larger city objectives, thus ensuring that common targets are met effectively. Similarly, collaborations that link safety efforts to economic growth highlight the mutual advantages realized when different entities work together. Training exercises with the police department exemplify how inter-departmental trust is built, enhancing operational efficiency and public confidence in emergency services. These initiatives underscore a fundamental strategy: cooperation enhances both morale and performance.

Further, the chapter emphasized transparency and inclusivity as key components in shaping trust between the community and local services. Regular town hall meetings offer a platform for open communication, allowing citizens to actively participate in discussions. This approach ensures alignment between departmental goals and community expectations, fostering a sense of shared responsibility. Commitment to diversity within the fire department strengthens this bond by reflecting the community it serves. Additionally, engaging residents through disaster preparedness workshops empowers them with critical skills while reinforcing their trust in local emergency services. Such efforts underscore the vital role that strong relationships play in effective leadership and public safety.

Chapter 6: Chief Neal's Quest

Reliable Medical Transport Service

Chief Neal's quest to establish a reliable medical transport service for Balch Springs demanded perseverance and strategic insight. With the primary ambulance provider failing to meet the city's evolving needs, Chief Neal faced the daunting challenge of spearheading change. The safety and welfare of the community were at stake, pressing him into action to find a solution that would restore trust and efficiency in emergency services. This chapter delves into the meticulous efforts he invested in crafting a Request for Qualifications (RFQ), one robust enough to attract capable providers committed to serving the city's unique demands. Drawing from experiences across similar municipalities, Chief Neal charted a course aimed at overcoming previous setbacks and ushering in improvements.

Throughout the narrative, readers will gain an understanding of the complex process Chief Neal navigated while meticulously drafting the RFQ. The chapter illuminates the critical elements involved, capturing the careful balance he maintained between local specifications and compliance with broader regulatory frameworks. The journey unfolds as Chief Neal consults experts, avoids pitfalls, and considers innovative solutions tailored to Balch Springs' distinct characteristics. Furthermore, it highlights his dedication to ensuring transparent communication and collaboration between providers and the fire department. By laying out this comprehensive path, the chapter prepares readers to appreciate the subsequent phases of evaluating bids and establishing a cornerstone partnership crucial for redefining healthcare accessibility within the community.

Drafting and Customizing the Request for Qualifications (RFQ)

In the pursuit of securing a reliable medical transport service for Balch Springs, Chief Neal embarked on a comprehensive journey to develop a Request for Qualifications (RFQ) that would attract the most capable providers. Understanding the significance of this task, he began by studying the RFQs from cities with similar demographics and challenges. This research illuminated effective structures and essential elements that could be tailored to meet the specific needs of Balch Springs. By examining these documents, Chief Neal gained insights into what had worked for other municipalities, allowing him to draw lessons both in terms of what constituted success and where pitfalls might lie.

Crafting an RFQ requires astute attention to detail, especially when addressing the unique features of a locale like Balch Springs. The city's specific demands included its geographical location, distinct traffic patterns, and diverse demographic challenges. These factors were critical in shaping an RFQ that was not only comprehensive but also highly customized. Chief Neal carefully considered how each element of the city's landscape affected emergency response times and service efficiency. For instance, the proximity of major highways and residential areas required strategic planning to ensure timely access to all neighborhoods, thereby mitigating any delays in emergency response.

An equally important component of the RFQ was to lay down clear expectations regarding communication and coordination between the fire department and the service provider. Past experiences had shown that miscommunication could lead to inefficiencies and poor service delivery. To counter this, Chief Neal emphasized the need for robust communication protocols within the RFQ. This approach aimed to foster seamless interactions, ensuring that the provider would work in tandem with local emergency services, rather than operate in isolation. Such collaboration is vital in enhancing the overall effectiveness of emergency responses and elevating community trust in the system.

Recognizing the complexities involved in drafting such an intricate document, Chief Neal sought legal consultations to ensure compliance with existing regulations. The importance of upholding rigorous standards while promoting open competition was paramount, as it ensured that no competent provider would be inadvertently excluded from the bidding process. Legal experts provided guidance on balancing these attributes—ensuring that the RFQ not only met legislative requirements but also served as a fair and competitive platform for potential service providers.

Drafting the RFQ required meticulous attention and dedication. With the guidance of experts and his own research findings, Chief Neal developed a comprehensive guideline for crafting an RFQ document. This guideline encompassed key steps such as defining clear objectives, identifying mandatory qualifications, and specifying evaluation criteria. By doing so, Chief Neal ensured that the RFQ was both detailed and adaptable, appealing to a wide range of qualified bidders who could genuinely address the needs of Balch Springs.

Customizing the RFQ further involved intricately understanding Balch Springs' unique characteristics. The city's demographic makeup posed certain challenges, such as language diversity and varying socio-economic conditions, which needed to be addressed in service provision. Incorporating these considerations into the RFQ allowed prospective bidders to present solutions explicitly tailored to the city's specific context, demonstrating their capacity to provide inclusive and efficient services to all residents.

Ensuring legal compliance remained a cornerstone in Chief Neal's strategy as he moved forward with the RFQ development. This step was crucial not only in safeguarding the integrity of the procurement process but also in enhancing accountability and transparency. By engaging with experienced legal advisors, Chief Neal was able to navigate the intricate web of regulatory demands seamlessly. This collaboration ensured that the RFQ did not impose excessive constraints, nor did it favor any particular entity, thereby fostering a competitive yet fair environment for all stakeholders.

Ultimately, the creation of an RFQ that accurately reflected the needs and aspirations of Balch Springs was an undertaking that required not just technical expertise but also a deep understanding of the community it aimed to serve. Chief Neal's dedication and strategic approach illustrated his commitment to resolving the significant challenge of acquiring a dependable ambulance service. His proactive steps set the stage for transformative improvements within the city's emergency services framework, aligning it with the overarching goal of enhancing public safety and welfare.

Evaluating Bids and Establishing a New Partnership

In his pivotal quest to secure a reliable medical transport service for Balch Springs, Chief Neal was faced with the daunting task of assessing bids and selecting a suitable ambulance service provider. Despite a limited pool of options, with only two bids submitted, the choice became clear as MJ Company distinguished itself through competitive pricing coupled with innovative proposals. This combination provided a strong foundation on which Chief Neal could build confidence in their ability to serve the community effectively.

MJ Company's proposal did not merely hinge on the basics of meeting operational needs. Instead, it included a pledge to station multiple ambulances within the city limits. This strategic placement promised to significantly enhance response times—a critical factor in emergency medical services where every second counts. The company's commitment went beyond simple logistics; they articulated plans for additional community benefits aimed at elevating the overall service quality. Their approach demonstrated an understanding that prompt medical attention is more than just a race against time; it's about ensuring comprehensive care and forging a deep connection with the community they aim to serve.

The process leading to MJ Company's selection was thorough and meticulous. Chief Neal understood that selecting an appropriate provider went beyond reviewing numbers on a page; it required a deeper dive into what each company could genuinely bring to the table. This exhaustive evaluation involved weighing numerous factors, from reliability and reputation to innovation and community engagement. MJ Company's bid stood out not only because of the concrete promises but also due to their dedicated efforts to understand the unique landscape and needs of Balch Springs. By choosing a partner willing to align closely with the city's vision for enhanced emergency medical services, Chief Neal ushered in a new era for healthcare accessibility in the area.

A significant part of MJ Company's allure was their proactive engagement and evident eagerness to form a partnership that transcends a conventional service agreement. They showcased a robust commitment to exceeding expectations by involving themselves actively in community initiatives and dialogues. This was not just about checking off contractual obligations; it reflected an earnest desire to improve safety standards and foster trust. Through educational programs and collaborative events, MJ Company portrayed themselves as a steadfast ally to the residents of Balch Springs, demonstrating that their role went beyond being a mere service provider.

Moreover, MJ Company's model included integrating technology in ways that promised not just efficiency but a forward-thinking approach to emergency medical services. Their proposals included innovations designed to streamline operations, reduce response times further, and ensure that crews were equipped with the latest training and resources. This progressive stance aligned well with Chief Neal's vision of cultivating a responsive and adaptable health service infrastructure—one that is fit to meet current demands and poised to rise to future challenges.

This transformative choice marked a shift towards greater accountability and transparency in service delivery. MJ Company's influence extended across various aspects of the city's emergency service provision, setting new benchmarks for quality and responsiveness. By instilling systems that allowed for real-time data tracking and community feedback loops, they ensured that improvements were not static but dynamically adjusted based on the evolving needs of Balch Springs residents.

As the relationship between the city and MJ Company strengthened, the tangible benefits began to manifest. The presence of readily available emergency vehicles strategically placed around the city profoundly improved not just statistical response times but also the perceived safety and security among residents. Community members began to see MJ Company not just as responders in times of crisis but as integral parts of their everyday lives, contributing positively to public health education and awareness campaigns.

Chief Neal's journey, while challenging, exemplified the potency of strategic partnerships in transforming essential services. It underscored the significance of fostering relationships that are mutually beneficial and focused on long-term community welfare. The collaboration between Balch Springs and MJ Company is a testament to how thoughtful decision-making can lead to incremental changes that reverberate across a community, enhancing quality of life and building resilient health service networks.

Final Thoughts

Chief Neal's journey in securing a dependable ambulance service for Balch Springs was marked by dedication and strategic foresight. By meticulously crafting the Request for Qualifications (RFQ), he ensured that it addressed the city's unique needs, from specific traffic patterns to diverse demographics. His approach was rooted in thorough research, legal compliance, and a keen understanding of the community's landscape, which set the stage for selecting a provider that could deliver effective emergency services. This process also highlighted the importance of clear communication and collaboration between the fire department and the chosen service provider, aiming to improve response times and enhance public trust.

Selecting MJ Company as the new ambulance service provider marked a turning point for Balch Springs, embodying a commitment to more than just operational efficiency. Their bid surpassed expectations with competitive pricing, innovative ideas, and a community-oriented approach. Chief Neal's thorough evaluation considered reliability, reputation, and the potential for meaningful community engagement, ultimately choosing a partner aligned with the city's vision. MJ Company's proactive involvement, technological integration, and focus on public health education underscored a shared goal of improving safety standards and building resilient health service networks. Through this partnership, tangible improvements in emergency response and community welfare began to unfold, demonstrating the power of thoughtful decision-making in advancing essential services.

Chapter 7: I.C.S. at It's Best

Strategies for Effective Incident Command

Managing incidents effectively is a critical skill that requires precision and coordination. Chief Neal's strategies for incident command demonstrate a remarkable blend of leadership and organization aimed at achieving efficient and effective responses in various situations. When an incident arises, the immediate challenge is to ensure all responding units work seamlessly together, despite coming from different backgrounds and specializations. In this complex environment, Chief Neal emphasizes the importance of clear communication channels to prevent misunderstandings and ensure everyone involved shares a common goal. His approach highlights how unified efforts can turn potentially chaotic scenarios into streamlined operations.

At the core of this chapter lies a detailed exploration of Chief Neal's distinctive methods, which serve as a roadmap for navigating the intricate landscape of incident management. The discussion begins by dissecting the principles of unity of command and unified command, which are vital for maintaining order and reducing confusion in multi-agency responses. These concepts are complemented by guidelines that not only standardize language but also establish clear roles and responsibilities among team members. Additionally, the chapter delves into the significance of adaptability in guidelines, stressing the need for flexibility when applying predefined rules to dynamic situations. By focusing on these elements, readers gain insights into the practical implementations that enhance operational success, foster teamwork, and improve overall safety during emergency responses.

Clear Communication and Unified Command

In the realm of incident command, effective communication and unified command stand as pillars of success. Chief Neal's approach underscores the significance of clear dialogue in orchestrating incident responses. The foundation of this strategy is the use of concise and standardized language. This practice fosters a shared understanding, or "common operating picture," among all teams involved. Imagine an emergency where responders from various units speak different jargon—chaos would be inevitable. By promoting a universal language, Chief Neal ensures that everyone interprets updates and instructions uniformly, reducing errors and enhancing operational efficiency.

A key aspect of Chief Neal's methodology is the implementation of 'unity of command.' This principle dictates that each individual in the field should have only one direct supervisor. Clear supervision channels eliminate confusion and overlap, providing precise direction during high-pressure situations. For instance, in a multi-agency response to a wildfire, having singular command lines means firefighters receive consistent instructions, minimizing miscommunication. Unity of command not only streamlines operations but also contributes to the safety and morale of the team, knowing they are guided with certainty.

Chief Neal further champions the concept of 'unified command,' especially when incidents span across multiple jurisdictions or involve several agencies. Unified command facilitates collaboration by integrating the resources and expertise of all parties involved. In practical terms, this might involve local law enforcement, federal agencies, and fire departments working together in a joint effort to handle a natural disaster. Unified command prevents duplication of efforts and leverages the strengths of each agency, leading to a more robust and cohesive response.

To ensure that these strategies succeed, clear roles and responsibilities must be established. Defining who does what is critical to fostering teamwork and maintaining accountability within the response team. Consider an earthquake scenario involving emergency medical services, search and rescue teams, and utility repair crews. When each group knows its specific duties and whom to report to, the operation runs smoothly with minimal friction. Accountability in roles not only improves efficiency but also builds trust among teams, as members see that everyone's contributions are valued and essential.

Guidelines can serve as a valuable tool in achieving effective communication and unified command. Establishing protocols for language use and command structures ensures consistency and clarity across all incidents. For example, developing a glossary of standardized terms and phrases helps decode complex information swiftly, aiding in quick decision-making. Likewise, setting up guidelines for leadership hierarchies aids in maintaining order during multifaceted responses.

However, it's important to note that guidelines must be adaptable. Every incident presents unique challenges, and strict adherence to rigid rules can be counterproductive. Flexibility allows incident commanders to adjust their strategies as circumstances evolve, ensuring responsiveness to unforeseen developments. Chief Neal's approach suggests balancing well-defined procedures with the agility to adapt, thus keeping incident command both efficient and resilient.

Strategic Planning and Continuous Improvement

In the realm of incident command, Chief Neal's approach emphasizes the importance of strategic planning and learning from past experiences. These elements are crucial for ensuring effective response and management during critical situations.

A key component within this strategy is the development of adaptive Incident Action Plans (IAPs). An IAP serves as a blueprint for responding to incidents by outlining objectives, strategies, and resource deployments. To be effective, these plans must be flexible enough to adapt to continually changing circumstances. This requires an acute awareness of situational dynamics coupled with a proactive mindset, ready to adjust tactics as new information becomes available. For instance, during a natural disaster, initial assumptions about the scope of damage may evolve rapidly. An adaptive IAP allows teams to recalibrate their priorities and actions in real-time, ensuring that efforts remain aligned with the most pressing needs.

Equally important to adaptive planning is efficient resource management. Effective incident command hinges on the wise allocation of personnel and equipment. It's not just about having resources; it's about using them intelligently. Decisions should be informed by a thorough assessment of the situation at hand, acknowledging both immediate and potential challenges. Imagine a fire department tackling a major wildfire—without careful coordination of firefighting resources and manpower, containment efforts might falter. Thus, leaders must continuously evaluate resource deployment and make strategic adjustments to maintain operational effectiveness.

Training and drills play an indispensable role in fortifying response capabilities. Regular practice sessions and simulations are akin to rehearsal in theater. They provide responders with practical experience, helping to cement protocols and procedures into muscle memory. During a simulated crisis, teams can test their communication lines, execute standard operating procedures, and identify areas for improvement. By recreating different scenarios, responders gain confidence and competence, which prove invaluable when real incidents unfold. Furthermore, this preparedness training offers room to explore innovative approaches and bolster teamwork—a key factor in handling high-pressure situations successfully.

Once an incident concludes, after-action reviews become the pathway to continuous improvement. This reflective process involves deconstructing what transpired, assessing the effectiveness of actions taken, and identifying both successes and shortcomings. The goal of an after-action review is twofold: self-reflection and shared learning. It provides a space where involved parties can honestly evaluate their performance, gaining insights that can refine future strategies. Such reviews could highlight overlooked aspects or unanticipated challenges, prompting revisions to existing plans or protocols. By documenting and sharing these insights, organizations build a collective knowledge base that enhances future preparedness.

Situational Awareness acts as the lifeline in every incident command operation. It involves maintaining a clear understanding of unfolding events while anticipating potential developments. Commanders need guidelines to sharpen situational awareness, such as consistently monitoring environmental changes and communicating effectively with other team members. This vigilance ensures that decision-makers have a comprehensive picture, enabling them to direct operations efficiently.

Overall, these elements outlined—adaptive plans, resource management, training, and reflective practices—work synergistically to elevate the quality of incident command. They transform theoretical constructs into tangible outcomes that save lives and mitigate damage. By anchoring his approach in strategic foresight and experiential learning, Chief Neal demonstrates how preparation and adaptability underpin successful incident management.

Final Thoughts

In this chapter, we've delved into Chief Neal's multifaceted approach to incident command, highlighting the importance of leadership skills, clear communication, and effective resource management. Chief Neal emphasizes using concise language to ensure a common understanding among all team members, which is pivotal during emergency responses. Through strategies like 'unity of command' and 'unified command,' he ensures that operations are streamlined, minimizing confusion while enhancing safety and morale. By integrating different agencies and clearly defining roles and responsibilities, Chief Neal creates an environment where teamwork thrives, and accountability becomes second nature.

Moreover, strategic planning and continuous improvement are crucial underpinnings of Chief Neal's philosophy. Adaptive Incident Action Plans and efficient resource management allow teams to quickly respond to evolving situations. Regular training and drills help responders refine their skills and cement protocols, preparing for real-life scenarios. After-action reviews further enable learning from past events, continually refining strategies for future incidents. By maintaining situational awareness and fostering a culture of reflection and growth, Chief Neal demonstrates how preparedness and adaptability lead to successful incident management, ultimately saving lives and reducing harm in critical situations.

Chapter 8: Managing Resources

Budgets, Equipment, and Staffing

Managing resources within a fire department is a complex task demanding strategic insight and prudent decision-making. It calls for an adept leader who can navigate the intricacies of budgeting, equipment maintenance, and staffing to ensure the department operates efficiently and effectively. This chapter delves into the resource management strategies implemented by Chief Neal at the Balch Springs Fire Department. Stepping into his leadership role, Chief Neal faced the formidable challenge of developing a comprehensive budget in a short timeframe. His approach required balancing financial constraints with operational priorities, all while maintaining the safety and readiness of his firefighting team. This chapter explores these challenges and presents the multifaceted solutions that emerged under his guidance.

As you explore this chapter, you will gain insight into Chief Neal's methodology of conducting detailed assessments and implementing strategic budgeting techniques. These strategies not only aligned with immediate fiscal needs but also supported long-term departmental goals. The narrative captures how he prioritized critical aspects like training and equipment maintenance, demonstrating effective fund allocation crucial to the department's success. By fostering a collaborative environment, Chief Neal engaged his team in dialogue about budgetary concerns, nurturing a sense of shared responsibility and innovative problem-solving. Moreover, his embrace of technological advancements and pursuit of external funding sources illustrates a forward-thinking mindset aimed at optimizing available resources. Through partnerships and grant acquisition, Chief Neal enhanced the department's capabilities, ensuring a resilient and adaptable framework to face modern-day challenges. This chapter offers an extensive exploration of these resource management strategies, providing readers with valuable lessons applicable to their professional challenges.

Strategic Budgeting and Resource Allocation

When Chief Neal assumed leadership of the Balch Springs Fire Department, he faced an immediate challenge: to develop a comprehensive budget in just two months. This daunting task required not only swift action but also strategic foresight. In tackling this hurdle, Chief Neal demonstrated effective resource management by employing strategies that would serve as a foundation for fiscal prudence and organizational efficiency.

The first step in his approach was conducting a thorough assessment of the department's financial landscape. This entailed analyzing past expenditure patterns, evaluating revenue streams, and identifying areas where costs could be sensibly reduced without compromising operational readiness. The focus on financial landscapes allowed him to understand the fiscal outlook and make informed decisions that aligned with both short-term needs and long-term goals. By understanding the nuances of the department's financial health, he could pinpoint opportunities to optimize spending and identify priority areas that demanded attention.

A significant aspect of Chief Neal's budgeting strategy was prioritizing essential needs, specifically training and equipment maintenance, over non-critical expenditures. His philosophy revolved around the belief that investing in core capabilities would provide the best return on investment while ensuring the safety and efficacy of firefighting operations. Training programs were deemed indispensable, as they equipped firefighters with the skills needed to perform their duties effectively and safely. Additionally, maintaining equipment to the highest standards ensured reliability during emergencies, significantly impacting the department's performance and success rate in critical situations.

To balance meeting a tight budget deadline, Chief Neal adhered to certain guiding principles aimed at ensuring efficient fund allocation and management. He implemented a guideline-driven approach to help determine which expenses were considered vital and which could be deferred or minimized. For instance, guidelines focused on aligning expenses with strategic priorities, assessing cost-benefit scenarios for each item, and considering the potential risks associated with reducing funding in specific areas. This structured method not only streamlined decision-making processes but also reinforced transparency and accountability within the organization.

Integrating transparent communication into budget development became another cornerstone of Chief Neal's methodology. Engaging team members from various levels in dialogue about budgetary constraints and expectations fostered a collaborative environment. By sharing insights and soliciting input from colleagues, Chief Neal cultivated a sense of shared responsibility, empowering individuals to contribute ideas and perspectives that could lead to innovative solutions. This participatory approach-built trust and encouraged collective ownership, enhancing commitment toward achieving departmental objectives despite financial limitations.

Moreover, embracing technological advancements proved valuable in supporting Chief Neal's resource management strategy. As part of his forward-thinking initiative, he explored potential grants and funding sources that could offset budgetary pressures. By securing external support for equipment upgrades or specialized projects, the department could preserve its internal resources for core activities like training or emergency response capabilities. This proactive pursuit of supplementary funds underscored his dedication to optimizing available assets while maximizing operational capacity.

Enhanced Resource Acquisition and Maintenance

Chief Neal's tenure at the Balch Springs Fire Department marked a transformative period in upgrading equipment and maintaining high operational standards. One of his notable achievements was securing $200,000 in grants aimed at modernizing firefighting equipment. This impressive feat not only enhanced the department's capabilities but also emphasized the critical importance of safety and efficiency improvements.

By successfully acquiring these grants, Chief Neal could implement substantial upgrades to the existing equipment. Such modernization efforts are vital as they significantly reduce risks associated with exposure to hazards that firefighters encounter. For instance, enhanced breathing apparatuses or improved thermal imaging cameras enable firefighting personnel to respond more effectively and safely during emergencies. The infusion of these funds allowed for the strategic acquisition of advanced tools, ensuring that each firefighter is well-equipped to confront the diverse challenges posed by modern-day fire incidents.

In parallel with equipment modernization, Chief Neal prioritized routine maintenance to ensure the reliability and extended life expectancy of essential apparatus like the brush truck. Routine maintenance is often overlooked in many departments due to time constraints or budget limitations; however, it plays a crucial role in preventing malfunctions during critical operations. By maintaining rigorous schedules and checklists, the department under Chief Neal's leadership ensured that each vehicle and piece of equipment remained in optimal condition. This commitment to regular upkeep not only minimized downtime but also maximized the operational availability of resources at all times.

To further align equipment purchases with the practical needs of the department, Chief Neal engaged firefighting personnel in the selection process. Involving team members who actively use the equipment fosters ownership and morale among the staff. It ensures that those who face day-to-day hazards have input into what tools would best support their efforts. When personnel feel that their insights and experiences are valued, it creates an environment of trust and collaboration. This inclusive approach also enhances the likelihood of successful integration and effective use of new technology, as firefighters are more inclined to adopt tools they helped choose.

Demonstrating a proactive and cooperative approach, Chief Neal also focused on cultivating partnerships and pursuing additional grants to enhance departmental resources. Establishing collaborations with other agencies and organizations broadens the scope of available opportunities for resource acquisition. Through such partnerships, the department could participate in joint training exercises, share innovations, and even access shared funding prospects. This network-driven strategy not only diversified the department's resource stream but also fostered an adaptable and resilient response framework.

Guidelines for securing necessary fire apparatus are pivotal to maintaining an efficient and responsive department. Under Chief Neal's guidance, the department showcased sound practices in identifying funding opportunities, drafting compelling proposals, and managing grant applications meticulously. These steps ensured that financial resources were allocated appropriately and aligned with strategic growth objectives.

Routine maintenance, particularly when faced with time pressures, requires diligent adherence to protocols and procedures. Developing a systematic checklist tailored specifically for different apparatus types can streamline this process. Assigning specific roles and responsibilities to team members eliminates ambiguity and promotes accountability in maintaining the equipment properly and efficiently.

Deliberative upgrades form another cornerstone of sustainable operational excellence. Taking measured steps involves thorough assessments of current equipment functionalities and anticipated advancements. By weighing the benefits of potential upgrades against budgetary constraints and operational demands, departments can strategically plan investments without overextending financial resources.

Nurturing professional growth within the department is equally crucial, especially under the pressures inherent in emergency services. Training programs that incorporate evolving techniques and technologies help equip personnel with the skills needed to adapt to changing environments. Continuous learning fosters confidence and strengthens cohesion within the team, ultimately contributing to the department's overarching success.

Finally, balancing workload effectively in high-pressure scenarios is essential to maintaining a well-functioning operation. Establishing work-life balance and manageable shift rotations can prevent burnout and fatigue among firefighters. Encouraging open communication and feedback regarding scheduling concerns enables leadership to address any issues promptly, fostering an environment where staff feels supported and valued.

Summary and Reflections

Under Chief Neal's leadership, the Balch Springs Fire Department has exemplified innovative resource management and strategic budgeting. Through a disciplined approach, Chief Neal assessed the department's financial standing, identifying key areas for efficiency without compromising safety or readiness. This chapter sheds light on how prioritizing essential needs over non-essential expenditures ensured that critical operations like training and equipment maintenance remained robust. By engaging team members in dialogue around budget constraints and involving them actively in decisions, Chief Neal fostered a sense of shared responsibility and collaboration that strengthened the department's operational capacity.

Furthermore, Chief Neal's focus on embracing technological advancements and securing grants was pivotal in modernizing the department's equipment and enhancing overall safety. His proactive stance in pursuing external funding sources not only preserved internal resources but also empowered firefighters with state-of-the-art tools to effectively tackle modern-day challenges. The participatory approach in equipment selection enriched trust within the team, encouraging a seamless adoption of new technologies. Through these strategies, Chief Neal has underscored the importance of resilient resource management, setting a precedent for optimizing assets while maintaining high standards of service in challenging times.

Chapter 9: Emergencies and Community

Emergency Response and Community Safety

Emergency response and community safety are integral aspects of any fire department's operations, demanding a well-coordinated strategy to protect lives and property. Within the Balch Springs Fire Department, led by Chief Neal, these elements form the foundation of their dedicated service to the community. As the chapter unfolds, it invites readers to look closer at how the department not only remains vigilant around the clock but also tackles the time-sensitive nature of emergencies with remarkable preparedness and efficiency. The leadership of Chief Neal is pivotal in this regard, having ingrained a culture of readiness throughout the department that transcends mere training exercises and drills.

The ensuing chapter delves into the multifaceted approach adopted by the Balch Springs Fire Department under Chief Neal's stewardship. It explores strategies ranging from fostering inter-agency cooperation to leveraging modern technology. Readers will gain insight into the seamless integration with other local emergency services which enhances response coordination during crises. Through an examination of the comprehensive training programs and community engagement initiatives, the chapter reveals how Chief Neal empowers both the firefighters and the public alike. Additionally, the focus on technology showcases the department's commitment to staying ahead of emerging challenges. This chapter promises to illuminate the meticulous planning and dynamic execution that characterize the department's commendable efforts in ensuring community safety and effective emergency response.

A 24/7 Promise: Always Ready to Respond & The Critical

Minutes: A Race Against Time

Under Chief Neal's leadership, the Balch Springs Fire Department has demonstrated an exceptional level of preparedness and response capability. One of the cornerstones of this prowess is the culture of readiness that Chief Neal ingrained in every member of the department. This is not merely a passive state but a dynamic commitment to ensure all personnel are perpetually primed for action. Through a systematic approach involving rigorous training sessions and regular drills, firefighters are equipped to confront emergencies with well-honed skills and strategic forethought. These exercises cultivate muscle memory essential for swift and effective responses, ensuring that each member knows their role intimately when seconds count.

The emphasis on coordination across various emergency agencies further underscores Chief Neal's commitment to optimizing response times during crises. Recognizing that collaboration is crucial for successful emergency management, Chief Neal has forged strong alliances with local police, medical services, and other first responders. This seamless integration facilitates immediate information sharing, resource allocation, and strategic planning, which can spell the difference between chaos and control in high-pressure situations. By fostering these inter-agency relationships, Chief Neal ensures that the department can efficiently mobilize collective efforts to address complex incidents, thereby enhancing public safety.

In addition to fostering human connections, Chief Neal also prioritizes technological advancement within the department. Modern technology serves as a vital tool in navigating emergencies effectively. Under his guidance, the fire department has been equipped with cutting-edge tools and technology. These innovations range from advanced communication systems to efficient dispatch protocols and state-of-the-art equipment capable of tackling diverse challenges, from structural fires to hazardous material spills. With well-maintained resources at their disposal, the team can respond to emergencies with precision and confidence, reducing the likelihood of equipment failures during critical operations.

A pivotal aspect of the department's strategy under Chief Neal is the focus on decisive action during the early stages of any emergency. The initial minutes of a crisis are often when the outcome is determined, making speed and decisiveness paramount. Chief Neal emphasizes a proactive stance, empowering his team to make rapid assessments and decisions based on gathered intelligence and strategic directives. This approach minimizes the escalation of disasters and maximizes the potential for saving lives, demonstrating the importance of having a well-prepared team ready to act swiftly under pressure.

Training programs designed by Chief Neal do more than prepare firefighters for immediate dangers; they instill a mindset geared toward continuous improvement and anticipation of potential threats. Each exercise simulates real-world scenarios that challenge the team to adapt quickly and think critically, reinforcing their ability to manage unforeseen variables without hesitation. By doing so, the department remains agile in its operations, capable of adjusting strategies mid-response if necessary.

Moreover, the focus on inter-departmental drills and joint exercises with other services acts as a proving ground for effective cooperation and strategic planning. These exercises foster an understanding among different entities, creating a unified response framework that eliminates bureaucratic delays and miscommunications. In high-stakes situations where time is of the essence, such clarity and cohesion can prevent the situation from spiraling out of control, safeguarding both the community and emergency personnel.

The investment in technology is matched by an equally important commitment to maintaining these resources. Regular checks and updates ensure that all equipment remains operationally effective, preventing breakdowns that could jeopardize mission success. This meticulous attention to detail not only prolongs the lifespan of the equipment but also reinforces the department's readiness to tackle emergencies at a moment's notice.

Chief Neal's philosophy of decisive action extends beyond mere response; it embodies a holistic view of emergency prevention and risk mitigation. By advocating for thorough community engagement and awareness programs, he promotes a proactive stance that empowers residents with essential knowledge and skills. These initiatives, though covered in depth elsewhere, underscore Chief Neal's comprehensive approach to emergency management, focusing on minimizing hazards before they develop into full-fledged crises.

The collective impact of these measures is evident in the department's exemplary track record. Under Chief Neal's direction, response times have improved significantly, and the effectiveness of interventions has increased, leading to heightened community trust and assurance in the department's capabilities. His leadership style inspires confidence not only within the department but also across the broader community, reflecting a deep-seated commitment to public safety and service excellence.

Community Involvement: Beyond Emergencies & Training for Excellence: Prepared for Every Scenario

The Balch Springs Fire Department, under the leadership of Chief Neal, has set forth a vision centered on proactive community engagement and excellence in training. A central strategy has been the implementation of comprehensive educational programs and safety drills aimed at empowering residents. By focusing on these initiatives, the department fosters a culture of community self-reliance, encouraging individuals to take an active role in ensuring their own safety during emergencies.

Through these programs, residents are equipped with vital knowledge about fire prevention, first aid, and how to respond effectively in various emergency scenarios. For instance, community workshops have been organized to teach evacuation procedures, the use of fire extinguishers, and basic CPR. These sessions are designed to be engaging yet informative, utilizing interactive methods such as live demonstrations and hands-on practice. The overarching goal is not just to disseminate information but to instill confidence in residents, so they feel prepared to act decisively when confronted with emergencies.

Beyond educating the public, Chief Neal's approach places a significant emphasis on the continuous professional development of firefighters. By prioritizing skill enhancement and certification in specialized areas like hazardous materials handling or advanced rescue operations, the department ensures its members are well-equipped to handle complex situations. Regular training sessions and workshops are tailored to address both fundamental firefighting techniques and emerging challenges in the field.

This commitment to growth is evident in the department's encouragement for each firefighter to pursue certifications that align with their interests and departmental needs. Such an approach not only improves the collective skill set of the team but also enhances job satisfaction by supporting personal aspirations within the firefighting profession. Consequently, these efforts cultivate an environment where firefighters remain motivated and prepared to deliver high-quality service during every call to action.

Building robust partnerships with local stakeholders forms another cornerstone of the department's strategic plan. Collaborative outreach initiatives are organized to strengthen relationships and establish trust within the community. Working closely with schools, businesses, and local organizations, the fire department participates in events like open houses and safety fairs, creating opportunities for interaction and engagement. These occasions allow for direct communication with the public, breaking down barriers and fostering mutual understanding between the department and the community it serves.

Such collaborations often extend beyond mere participation at events. They involve long-term projects aimed at bolstering the overall safety infrastructure of the city. For example, partnering with educational institutions to develop disaster preparedness curriculums can prepare future generations with crucial survival skills. Similarly, working alongside local businesses to establish emergency response protocols helps ensure a swift and coordinated reaction to crises. Through these partnerships, the department not only strengthens its operational capabilities but also reinforces the notion that public safety is a shared responsibility.

Internally, Chief Neal promotes a collaborative environment within the department by advocating for mentorship and shared learning experiences among firefighters. Seasoned veterans are encouraged to mentor newer recruits, sharing their expertise and insights gained from years of service. This exchange of knowledge creates a dynamic learning ecosystem where all members benefit from diverse perspectives and experiences.

Regular debriefings after critical incidents serve as another platform for collaborative learning. During these sessions, team members reflect on their actions, discuss what went well, and identify areas for improvement. Such practices foster a culture of continuous learning and adaptation, enabling the department to evolve alongside the changing landscape of emergency response.

Final Thoughts

Under the guidance of Chief Neal, the Balch Springs Fire Department makes every effort to ensure readiness and responsiveness. Emphasizing a multifaceted strategy, the department integrates comprehensive training, inter-agency collaboration, and technological advancements.

This approach equips firefighters with the necessary skills and confidence for effective emergency response. These initiatives not only fortify the department's operational capabilities but also build public trust, reinforcing the community's safety.

Chief Neal's focus extends beyond immediate response to proactive community engagement and capacity building. Educational outreach and skill enhancement programs empower residents with essential knowledge, fostering self-reliance in crisis situations. Concurrently, partnerships with local stakeholders and collaborative learning within the department refine strategies and foster shared responsibility. Collectively, these efforts illustrate a commitment to excellence, ensuring the department serves as a pillar of safety and preparedness.

Chapter 10: Training for the Future

Training and Development for a Safer Tomorrow

Training and development for a safer tomorrow are paramount in shaping the operational landscape of emergency services. At the forefront of this endeavor is Chief Eric J. Neal, whose innovative approach to leadership and training at the Balch Springs Fire Department serves as a beacon for others in the field. His commitment to enhancing the department's operational capacity represents a dedication to not only improving response times and efficiency but also nurturing the skills and capabilities of each team member. By focusing on restructuring leadership roles and implementing specialized training programs, Chief Neal seeks to ensure that the community is well served by adept and capable professionals. This chapter delves into his transformative vision, highlighting how it steers the department towards achieving greater safety for all.

Diving into the core elements of Chief Neal's strategy, the chapter explores his structured realignment of leadership positions within the fire department. The introduction of roles such as Lieutenants and drivers marks a significant step in refining command dynamics and ensuring effective emergency operations. Furthermore, the chapter examines the comprehensive training and mentoring frameworks instituted to prepare personnel for these critical roles. Chief Neal's focus on continuous professional development and scenario-based training plays a key role in building the confidence and expertise required for tackling complex emergencies. Alongside real-world simulations and targeted skill enhancement, the chapter outlines how the department fosters a culture of adaptability, quick decision-making, and teamwork. Through examining the criteria for role selection and the emphasis on meritocracy and transparency, the narrative provides insights into how these practices bolster trust and motivation among the personnel. Ultimately, the reader will gain an understanding of Chief Neal's strategic initiatives aimed at ensuring leadership continuity and operational excellence within the Balch Springs Fire Department.

Restructuring for Enhanced Leadership

In the constantly evolving landscape of emergency response, transformational leadership remains crucial in ensuring that operations are both efficient and effective. Chief Eric J. Neal's vision for a safer tomorrow is grounded in restructuring the leadership hierarchy of the Balch Springs Fire Department to meet modern challenges head-on. A pivotal element of this transformation is the strategic introduction of Lieutenants and drivers as a means of improving leadership dynamics and operational efficiency.

Lieutenants represent an essential tier within this restructured leadership framework. As frontline leaders, they play a critical role not only in executing commands but also in ensuring strict adherence to established protocols. Their presence bridges the gap between operational demands and administrative oversight, which fosters a robust adherence to safety measures and efficient task execution. By mentoring junior personnel and providing guidance during high-stress situations, Lieutenants cultivate a team environment focused on safety and cohesion.

Moreover, effective lieutenancy is indispensable when navigating complex emergencies. For instance, in scenarios where quick decision-making can mean the difference between life and death, Lieutenants must be adept at assessing risks and deploying resources promptly. This capacity to lead decisively and ensure protocol adherence underscores their value in the hierarchy, while simultaneously nurturing future leaders through example and mentorship.

Introducing drivers into the department's operational strategy adds another dimension of readiness and efficiency. Tasked with managing transport logistics, drivers ensure that personnel and equipment arrive promptly at emergency sites. The role of the driver extends beyond mere transportation; it is an integral part of the strategic deployment and supply chain management vital for emergency responses. Efficient coordination of vehicle maintenance schedules, understanding optimal routes under different conditions, and working closely with dispatch centers all contribute to minimizing response times and enhancing mission success.

Furthermore, the realignment of the leadership structure acknowledges the dynamic needs of contemporary firefighting. The traditional hierarchical models, while foundational, need adaptation to accommodate the increasing complexity of emergencies in urban environments. This adaptation requires leaders who are not just well-versed in firefighting tactics but are also adept at leveraging technology and data-driven strategies to make informed decisions quickly.

Leadership realignment involves redefining roles and responsibilities to better reflect the diverse challenges firefighters face today. As such, Chief Neal's approach considers factors like population density, infrastructure changes, and emerging threats, aiming to create a more responsive and agile command structure. This foresight ensures the department is not only reactive but proactively anticipates potential hazards through enhanced situational awareness and strategic planning.

The guidelines for introducing Lieutenants and drivers are paramount to this transformation. Identifying individuals who demonstrate leadership potential and offering them targeted training and development programs helps facilitate a smooth transition into these roles. Ensuring that the selection process is merit-based and transparent builds trust and motivates personnel, setting a positive precedent for performance excellence.

In implementing these guidelines, the department invests in continuous professional development tailored to the unique pressures faced by Lieutenants and drivers. Regular workshops, scenario-based training sessions, and peer evaluations form a comprehensive support system enabling new leaders to thrive and innovate within their roles. Additionally, fostering open communication channels between experienced personnel and newcomers promotes knowledge sharing and experiential learning, further strengthening operational effectiveness.

Ultimately, this transformative approach positions the Balch Springs Fire Department as a paragon of modern emergency management. By prioritizing leadership realignment and strategic role development, Chief Neal not only addresses current operational inefficiencies but also lays the groundwork for sustained community safety practices. Leading by example, he demonstrates the importance of adaptive leadership in preparing for and overcoming the multifaceted challenges of an ever-changing world.

Strategic Training and Succession Planning

In the realm of public safety, training and development are crucial components in equipping personnel with robust skills and preparing them for future leadership roles. Chief Eric J. Neal's approach to leadership within the Balch Springs Fire Department exemplifies this by focusing on comprehensive training programs that cover a wide range of essential skills. By incorporating various aspects such as firefighting techniques, medical procedures, hazardous materials management, and command systems, the department ensures that its personnel are well-prepared for any emergency situation they might encounter.

A cornerstone of Chief Neal's strategy is the implementation of strategic training initiatives, designed to not only enhance operational capacity but also foster personal growth among team members. These initiatives integrate real-world scenarios, allowing firefighters to experience and navigate potential challenges in a controlled environment. By simulating high-pressure situations, trainees can build confidence and proficiency in their skills, ensuring they are ready when real emergencies arise. Guidelines for these training exercises emphasize adaptability, quick decision-making, and teamwork, critical components for effective firefighting and rescue operations.

Professional development is another key aspect of this transformative approach. The encouragement of obtaining certifications and enrolling in specialized courses allows personnel to deepen their knowledge and expertise in specific areas of interest or need. This not only bolsters individual careers but enhances the collective capabilities of the fire department. Firefighters are motivated to pursue advanced certifications in areas such as emergency medical services, technical rescue, and hazardous material response. By supporting continuous education, the department cultivates an environment where learning and improvement are ongoing processes.

Identifying and nurturing future leaders within the department requires a systematic approach to talent identification and readiness assessment. By evaluating individuals based on their performance, aptitude, and potential for growth, the department can strategically select candidates who exhibit strong leadership qualities. This process involves assessing both technical skills and interpersonal abilities, recognizing that effective leadership encompasses much more than operational competence alone. Prospective leaders are given various opportunities to demonstrate their capabilities in real-life settings, providing them with valuable experiences that contribute to their development.

Mentoring programs play a vital role in supporting emerging leaders as they transition into more significant responsibilities. Seasoned officers, with years of experience and wisdom, serve as mentors, guiding less experienced firefighters through the complexities of leadership roles. These mentoring relationships serve not only as educational tools but also as avenues for building trust and camaraderie within the department. Mentors share first-hand insights and knowledge, helping mentees navigate challenges and achieve personal and professional goals. Such programs ensure that the next generation of leaders is well-prepared to uphold the department's commitment to excellence and community safety.

The long-term impact of such comprehensive training and development initiatives is profound. Not only do they prepare firefighters for immediate challenges, but they also lay the groundwork for sustained leadership succession and departmental growth. As seasoned officers retire, the department benefits from a pipeline of capable, well-trained individuals who can step into leadership roles with confidence and competence. This approach mitigates the risks associated with leadership voids and ensures continuity in maintaining the safety and effectiveness of fire department operations.

Ultimately, the essence of Chief Neal's vision lies in empowering each member of the Balch Springs Fire Department to reach their utmost potential while simultaneously fostering a culture of learning, collaboration, and resilience. Through a combination of rigorous training programs, support for continued education, systematic talent identification, and supportive mentoring, the department not only enhances its operational readiness but also secures a prosperous future filled with highly capable leaders. It is this dedication to comprehensive preparation and forward-thinking that ensures the safety and well-being of the community, both today and in the years to come.

Core Message

Chief Eric J. Neal's leadership transformation within the Balch Springs Fire Department serves as a testament to his forward-thinking approach in enhancing community safety. His restructuring of the department focuses on introducing key roles, such as Lieutenants and drivers, which strengthen the operational capacity and leadership dynamics. By empowering personnel with new responsibilities and opportunities for growth, Chief Neal ensures that the department remains agile and prepared for modern emergencies. This focus on leadership realignment not only addresses the complexities of today's firefighting challenges but also nurtures future leaders through targeted mentorship and training.

Central to Chief Neal's strategy is the emphasis on strategic training and development. Comprehensive programs equip team members with essential skills, spanning from technical expertise in emergency situations to leadership readiness for future roles. The integration of real-world scenarios in training enhances the team's preparedness while promoting personal growth. This dedication to continuous education fosters an environment that values learning and improvement. Through detailed mentorship and talent assessment, the department identifies potential leaders and supports them in their career progression. Ultimately, these initiatives ensure sustained community safety by preparing well-trained individuals capable of leading the department with confidence and competence.

Chapter 11: The Balch Springs Fires

A Trial by Fire

Exploring the Balch Springs fires reveals a critical moment in time when routine life intersected with an unexpected natural disaster. These events unfolded during a period of intense heat and drought, creating conditions ripe for devastation. It began with what appeared to be a simple task, a mowing crew tending to dry grass, which unexpectedly became the catalyst for chaos. What happened next tested not only the firefighters' readiness but also highlighted the strength and determination of a community facing adversity. As flames spread swiftly, driven by unforgiving winds, the scene transformed into one requiring immediate strategic responses and unwavering courage.

This chapter delves into the multifaceted aspects of combating the Balch Springs fires. Readers will encounter detailed accounts of the challenges faced by firefighters as they battled against overwhelming odds and worked tirelessly to protect residential areas from the advancing blaze. The narrative also captures the urgent mobilization of resources and the strategic coordination required to contain the fire, involving not just local efforts but reinforcements from neighboring jurisdictions. Furthermore, it highlights the different elements of the community's response, illustrating how residents came together amid crisis, supported each other, and learned valuable lessons in resilience and recovery. Through this exploration, the chapter underscores the importance of preparation, cooperation, and adaptability in overcoming such formidable trials.

The Rapid Spread of the Fire

In the sweltering heat of a parched summer, the dry grass crackled like kindling beneath the relentless sun in Balch Springs. In such conditions, any spark could ignite a raging inferno, as was the case on that fateful day when a routine mowing task turned into an unforeseen catastrophe. The ignition point was simple enough—a mowing crew inadvertently created sparks while trimming grass in an area that had been scorched by drought, leaving it vulnerable to fire. These tiny embers found a perfect bed of tinder among the overgrown, desiccated brush, and within moments, flames leaped to life.

What began as small tongues of fire quickly transformed into an aggressive blaze, fanned by unyielding high winds that seemed determined to spread destruction. The wind carried the fire across fields with a speed and determination that left little time for a measured response. The brittle branches snapped and fed the growing fire, which began consuming everything in its path. Thick columns of smoke rose ominously into the sky, creating a tapestry of chaos and urgency that painted the horizon with an unsettling hue.

Faced with this burgeoning disaster, the local Fire Department sprang into action, but the odds were daunting from the start. The initial firefighters arriving on the scene were met with an inferno that exceeded the typical challenges faced in everyday emergencies. The sheer scale and velocity of the blaze were overwhelming; the flames moved with alarming rapidity and ferocity, almost as if the land itself were burning from within. This unexpected surge was more than just an assault on the terrain—it was a test of the firefighters' resolve and resourcefulness in the face of adversity.

The Fire Department's immediate concern was to strategize a defense against the imminent threat the fire posed to residential areas. Protecting lives and property became their foremost priority, the realization dawning quickly that containing the fire itself would require reinforcements and coordination beyond what was currently available. With embers snapping at the heels of homes, the firefighters directed their efforts to create firebreaks, attempting to halt the progression of the flames toward populated zones.

Yet, despite these valiant efforts, the situation demanded more than courage; it required adaptability and quick decision-making. The firefighters sought to contain the fire by using every resource at their disposal, including water hoses, fire-resistant foams, and earth-moving equipment, to barricade the communities from the advancing peril. However, the fire's behavior was unpredictable, challenging even the most seasoned veterans who battled it with everything they had.

Each moment brought new obstacles, from changing wind directions that threatened to redirect the fire towards other danger zones, to the exhaustion that crept in from hours of relentless work under harsh conditions. Coordination among the team was crucial, as was maintaining communication with community leaders to ensure evacuees received timely warnings. Firefighters rotated in shifts, not only to rest their weary bodies but also to maintain the stamina required for sustained combat against the blaze.

Amidst the chaos, stories of bravery emerged, painting a portrait of unity and dedication. Volunteers joined efforts alongside professionals, bolstering manpower and morale. It was a collective struggle against an enemy without conscience, driven by the shared goal of preserving life and livelihood. The firefighting units worked tirelessly, their engines roaring like lions in defiance, battling the elements and the clock.

Despite being initially overwhelmed, the Fire Department's swift prioritization and community-centric approach showcased a spirit of perseverance that hinted at hope. Ensuring the safety of neighborhoods and businesses involved quick cooperation and continuous reassessment of strategies. As fire lines were dug deeper and wider, water tankers replenished rapidly depleting resources, underscoring the need for an efficient logistical framework.

Throughout this trial by fire, the community learned invaluable lessons about preparation and resilience. The narrative of how the fire spread and the initial firefighting challenges served as both a cautionary tale and a testament to human endurance. It spoke volumes about the need for awareness and readiness in the face of potential environmental threats, emphasizing the importance of collaboration between municipal bodies, emergency services, and residents.

The balance between prevention and reaction was evident, as was the necessity for comprehensive emergency planning. While the ordeal highlighted gaps in immediate capacity, it also illuminated opportunities for improvement, driving home the message that preparedness could mitigate disaster impact significantly.

Coordinating Reinforcements and Fighting the Blaze

The sudden eruption of the Balch Springs fires was an unprecedented event that tested the limits of local firefighting capabilities. As flames engulfed more areas than anticipated, it became clear that the resources on hand were insufficient for the scale of the crisis. The urgency of the situation prompted an immediate call for reinforcements, with neighboring departments and specialized units summoned to provide necessary backup. This mobilization required not only speed but also precision, as any delay could result in further devastation.

With alarm bells ringing across multiple jurisdictions, fire departments from surrounding areas quickly responded to the call. The coordinated effort was nothing short of remarkable; dozens of engines and crews united with a singular mission—to stem the tide of destruction. However, bringing together forces from different districts was only the beginning. Each unit came with its own protocols and operational styles, necessitating seamless integration to maximize effectiveness.

Such collaboration meant engaging in thorough strategic planning. Leadership within various departments and emergency management personnel convened to craft a cohesive approach. This was not a straightforward task, as there were numerous logistical considerations, including the allocation of resources and the safety of both firefighters and residents. Planning discussions involved determining which areas demanded immediate attention and devising tactics that would leverage the strengths of each team involved. Coordination extended beyond just firefighting efforts, requiring close communication with law enforcement and medical teams to ensure comprehensive incident management.

A central element to handling the response effectively was establishing a command post. Situated strategically, this hub served as the nerve center for operations, providing a centralized location where leaders could monitor the unfolding situation and make quick decisions. Alongside the command post, setting up staging areas was critical to manage the influx of incoming units efficiently. These areas allowed for proper organization, ensuring that every piece of equipment and personnel was directed appropriately, avoiding chaos in an already volatile environment.

The command post operated around the clock, handling continuous updates and adjusting strategies accordingly. This dynamic approach was essential as fire conditions changed rapidly, sometimes shifting due to unexpected wind patterns or structural collapses. Within these centers of command, experienced officers utilized advanced technology alongside traditional methods, such as maps and radios, to maintain oversight and communicate directives clearly. The shared goal was to bring every available resource together cohesively to confront the immense challenge presented by the blaze.

Once the organizational framework was in place, attention turned towards executing a coordinated attack on the fire itself. Tackling an inferno of this magnitude required striking from multiple fronts.

Firefighters divided into specialized teams, each tasked with suppressing particular sectors of the wildfire. This division allowed them to concentrate efforts where they were most needed while also preventing the fire's spread to new areas. Such a strategy demanded precise timing and impeccable discipline, as there was little room for error when battling against nature's fury.

One key aspect of this multi-pronged assault was the usage of aerial support to complement ground efforts. Helicopters and planes released retardants from above, targeting hard-to-reach hotspots and easing the burden on crews navigating treacherous terrain below. Meanwhile, bulldozers cleared brush and created firebreaks, crucial in halting the fire's advance. This synergy between air and ground teams exemplified the kind of unified action that was necessary to make headway against the relentless flames.

Despite their best efforts, the path to containing the fire was fraught with obstacles. Weather conditions fluctuated unexpectedly, with shifting winds posing a continual threat to the stability of the fire lines. In addition, the sheer intensity of the heat proved daunting, pushing both men and machinery to their limits. As night fell, visibility issues added another layer of complexity, demanding heightened vigilance and reliance on spotlights and thermal imaging for guidance.

Throughout these trials, the steadfast dedication and professionalism of the responders shone through. Their determination was matched by the resilience of the community, whose unwavering support bolstered morale. Residents, though fearful for their homes and loved ones, rallied behind the responders, providing sustenance and encouragement during the grueling battle.

Community Impact and Recovery Efforts

In the wake of the Balch Springs fires, families found themselves grappling with the immediate aftermath of a disaster that upended their lives. The devastation left many homes either damaged or entirely destroyed, resulting in widespread displacement. Families who had lived in their neighborhoods for generations suddenly faced uncertainty about their future. The loss of a home is not just a physical deprivation; it represents the loss of security and stability—a hard reality for those affected. With nowhere to turn, these families yearned for support from their community and reassurance that recovery was possible.

Amidst this turmoil, local organizations and the Red Cross quickly mobilized to provide immediate relief. Coordinating aid and providing essential supplies became a priority. Shelters were established to accommodate displaced residents, offering a temporary refuge where they could regroup and plan their next steps. Food, clothing, and medical assistance were distributed systematically to ensure that no one was left without basic necessities. This effort required meticulous planning and execution as volunteers diligently worked to address the diverse needs of those impacted by the fires.

Guidelines were crucial during this phase to streamline aid distribution and make sure resources were used effectively. For example, prioritizing the most vulnerable populations such as children and the elderly ensured targeted support. Communication channels were also set up to keep everyone informed about available resources and services, helping alleviate some of the anxiety caused by uncertainty.

The community's role in recovery efforts cannot be overstated. In the face of adversity, the people of Balch Springs demonstrated remarkable resilience and solidarity. Donations poured in from individuals and businesses alike, funding initiatives to restore normalcy. Fundraisers rallied local residents and external supporters to contribute financially, each event reinforcing the spirit of unity amidst hardship. People volunteered their time and skills, whether it was helping clean up debris or offering professional expertise to rebuild homes.

Community gatherings became more than just fundraising events; they served as rallying points for hope and connection. Each volunteer and donor story added another layer to a shared narrative of resilience. The tales of neighbors helping neighbors fostered an atmosphere of collective effort, strengthening bonds between community members who might otherwise have remained strangers.

Beyond addressing material losses, the emotional and psychological toll on survivors needed attention. The trauma of losing everything in a matter of moments can be overwhelming, leading to stress, anxiety, and depression. Recognizing this, counseling services were made available to residents, offering a safe space to express fears and emotions. These sessions acknowledged the psychological impact of the disaster, equipping individuals with coping strategies as they navigated the road to recovery.

Community meetings played a critical role in fostering open communication and mutual support. These gatherings allowed residents to voice their concerns, share experiences, and seek advice from mental health professionals. Just the act of speaking candidly about their struggles helped lift some of the weight off their shoulders. The knowledge that others were undergoing similar trials provided comfort and camaraderie.

Through these efforts, the community of Balch Springs painted a portrait of resilience. They exemplified how combined determination, and compassion can overcome even the most daunting challenges. The lessons learned from their experiences highlight the importance of preparedness, unity, and empathy in crisis situations.

Lessons Learned

The chapter delves into the profound challenges faced during the Balch Springs fires, painting a vivid picture of both the ferocity of the flames and the bravery of those who confronted them. The narrative captures the fire's rapid spread and the immediate response by local firefighters, who battled tirelessly despite overwhelming conditions. Through detailed accounts of strategic efforts and relentless coordination among firefighting teams, the text reveals the extent of human dedication required to manage such an unpredictable disaster. The resilience of the community shines through as they rally together, supporting each other while striving to protect their homes and livelihoods.

Reflecting on these events highlights the strength found in unity and the essential role of preparation in crisis management. The collective efforts of firefighters, volunteers, and residents underscore the shared human ability to persevere against adversity. As the community faced the aftermath of destruction, their cooperative spirit paved the way for recovery and renewal. By addressing both immediate and long-term needs, they demonstrated the power of empathy and action. This chapter not only recounts a significant event but serves as a testament to the unwavering resolve that can emerge when individuals unite for a common goal.

Chapter 12: The Flood of 2022

A Dual Challenge

The Flood of 2022 in Balch Springs was a pivotal moment that tested the ingenuity and resilience of Chief Neal and his firefighting team. As the waters rose, transforming familiar streets into raging rivers, the team faced an entirely new set of circumstances. Their experience primarily lay in battling blazes; however, this unprecedented event demanded a rapid adaptation to water rescue operations. Chief Neal's leadership shone through as he guided his crew in meeting this dual challenge head-on, harnessing their skills and determination to confront nature's fury with courage and resolve. The floodwaters altered not just the physical landscape but also posed complex logistical and strategic problems that required innovative solutions.

In this chapter, readers will delve into the multifaceted challenges that emerged during the flood response, highlighting the remarkable adaptability displayed by the firefighters. It explores how the team redefined their strategies and tools to address immediate survival needs while planning for long-term recovery. The narrative will cover logistical shifts, such as the need for specialized equipment and retraining personnel, alongside the importance of ensuring safe evacuation routes amidst changing conditions. It also examines the critical role of effective communication and coordination among various agencies in managing the crisis. Through these stories, the chapter showcases how Chief Neal's forward-thinking approach and interagency collaboration were instrumental in navigating the dual threats of the flood, offering vital lessons in disaster preparedness and response.

The Challenges of Flood Response

The flood of 2022 presented a unique set of challenges for the firefighters in Balch Springs, under the guidance of Chief Neal. The historic floodwaters that engulfed the city were unprecedented and added a layer of complexity to emergency response efforts quite distinct from the typical demands of fighting wildfires. Unlike fires that are visible and somewhat predictable as they spread, floodwaters transform the landscape in unforeseen ways. Streets become rivers, landmarks disappear beneath murky currents, and the terrain becomes both unpredictable and perilous.

Navigating these submerged streets required an overhaul in the logistics strategies traditionally employed by the firefighting team. In typical rescue operations involving fire, first responders rely on standard vehicles and equipment engineered to withstand heat and access rough terrains. However, as the floodwaters rose, those familiar vehicles became inadequate. The need for specialized equipment such as boats, inflatable rafts, and life vests became starkly apparent. This shift necessitated not only immediate logistical changes but also foresight in procurement and maintenance of water-specific rescue tools. Implementing this equipment effectively required retraining personnel in their use, merging practical skills with strategic thinking to navigate safely through flooded areas.

Ensuring safe evacuation routes emerged as a critical priority. During a wildfire, pathways may close due to flames or smoke, which can often be anticipated and planned for in advance. Floodwaters, however, can cut off access without warning, leaving people stranded and unable to escape the rising tide. Establishing reliable routes for evacuation required firefighters to balance the immediate life-saving needs with longer-term recovery operations. Here, decision-making became crucial; determining when and how to evacuate residents without exposing them to unnecessary risks demanded a calculated approach focused on agility and adaptability. Practical guidelines the team followed included pre-assessment of vulnerable areas, continuous monitoring of water levels, and dynamic reevaluation of route accessibilities.

Effective communication and coordination among various agencies were essential to managing this crisis and minimizing public risk. The nature of flood rescues, dealing with displaced individuals and destroyed infrastructure, called for seamless interaction between the firefighting team, police, medical services, and local government. Each agency played a specific role within a larger framework designed to ensure community safety and resource allocation efficiency.

Coordination was further complicated by the necessity for real-time information sharing. The fast-paced evolution of flood conditions required accurate data dissemination, facilitated by technology, to all parties involved. This included tracking weather patterns, flooding forecasts, and status updates about the affected regions. Models of mutual aid and shared responsibilities allowed for the effective distribution of resources and manpower, thereby enhancing the response capabilities significantly. This cooperative strategy minimized duplication of efforts and focused collective energy on achieving the most pivotal outcomes.

Another layer of complexity lay in maintaining clear lines of communication with the citizens of Balch Springs. Amidst panic and uncertainty, providing timely and accurate information through various media outlets—social networks, radio broadcasts, and community hotlines—was vital in keeping the public informed and calm. An informed populace contributes substantially to orderly evacuations and compliance with safety directives, reducing inadvertent risks associated with misinformation or communication breakdowns.

Throughout the ordeal, it was evident that the multifaceted approach adopted by Chief Neal and his team served as a blueprint for future disaster responses. Addressing the challenges posed by the flood required more than tactical skill; it called for innovation, compassion, and resilience. The ongoing adaptation to new realities showcased the depth of preparedness and commitment of the Balch Springs firefighters, affirming the necessity for flexible strategy combined with a solid foundation of basic emergency response principles. Adjustments made during this time highlighted important lessons on the value of readiness for diverse types of emergencies, underscoring the importance of investing in comprehensive training programs and interagency partnerships.

Adaptability and Skill Transition

The flood of 2022 presented a formidable dual challenge to the firefighting team in Balch Springs, spearheaded by Chief Neal. Primarily trained to combat fires, the team faced a starkly different adversary: water. This sudden shift from fire suppression to water rescue required an immediate application of diverse skills fostered under Chief Neal's visionary leadership. It was a testament to the adaptability ingrained within the team, showcasing their capacity to pivot rapidly and effectively between disparate emergencies.

Under the astute guidance of Chief Neal, the firefighters of Balch Springs were not only adept at fighting blazes but had cultivated a proficiency in dealing with water-related emergencies. This adaptability was not born overnight but was a result of strategic foresight and comprehensive training regimens. The shift from responding to flames to navigating floodwaters underscored Chief Neal's emphasis on diversifying skill sets, preparing his team for any eventuality. Such forward-thinking leadership instilled confidence and competence among the crew, enabling them to manage the unpredictable nature of disasters.

Specialized training in swift water rescues became a cornerstone of the team's seamless transition during the floods. Prior sessions on handling swift currents, operating rescue boats, and efficiently using ropes allowed the firefighters to execute operations with precision and safety. For example, the swift deployment of inflatable rescue boats proved crucial in evacuating stranded residents from submerged homes. By integrating these specialized skills into their response framework, they ensured that even in unfamiliar waters, their actions were decisive and effective.

The proficiency demonstrated in these critical situations can be attributed to rigorous preparation through foresight. Chief Neal had long recognized the potential for natural disasters beyond fires and prioritized equipping his team with the requisite knowledge and tools. Training programs were crafted to simulate real-life scenarios involving both fire and water emergencies, ensuring team members were mentally and physically prepared. This level of preparedness enabled the firefighters to confront the dual challenges posed by the flood with remarkable efficiency, minimizing risk while maximizing rescue efforts.

Moreover, the versatility displayed by the team during this crisis highlighted the necessity for ongoing multi-hazard preparedness. In a world increasingly prone to natural disasters, the ability to shift seamlessly between different types of emergency response is invaluable. The firefighting team's adept handling of the situation underscored the importance of embracing a wide range of skills and knowledge areas. This approach not only safeguards communities but also enhances the resilience and capability of those tasked with protecting them.

In light of these experiences, it is clear that post-flood analysis and preparedness improvements must remain a priority. Reflecting on the operational successes and challenges encountered during the flood response provides valuable insights into areas needing enhancement. By reviewing their actions, the team can identify strengths to build upon and weaknesses to address, ultimately refining their strategies for future incidents.

A comprehensive guideline for improving preparedness could involve conducting regular assessments of current training protocols and equipment. Ensuring that all team members receive continual education in both fire and water rescue techniques will strengthen overall readiness. Furthermore, simulations that incorporate unexpected variables—such as simultaneous threats or resource limitations—can better prepare responders for complex scenarios.

Future strategies should also emphasize community engagement and education in disaster preparedness. Building a resilient community requires collaboration between emergency services and residents. Educating the public on evacuation procedures, safety measures, and emergency contacts prior to a disaster can significantly enhance collective response efforts. Establishing communication channels and facilitating workshops on disaster readiness can empower individuals to act swiftly and safely in the face of adversity.

By fostering a culture of preparedness and adaptability, the firefighting team in Balch Springs serves as a model for others facing similar challenges. Their experience during the flood of 2022 demonstrates that with the right leadership, training, and mindset, it is possible to overcome even the most daunting dual threats. As the climate continues to change, bringing with it a spectrum of risks, the lessons learned from these events will guide future generations in safeguarding their communities.

Community Support and Recovery Efforts

In the aftermath of the devastating flood of 2022, the role of the Balch Springs Fire Department extended far beyond their traditional firefighting duties. Under the guidance of Chief Neal, the department was instrumental in leading community recovery efforts, becoming a lifeline for residents seeking stability and support during one of the most challenging periods they had ever faced. Their involvement went beyond the initial heroic rescue operations, as they played a critical role in supporting community-led recovery initiatives and ensuring the efficient allocation of resources necessary for rebuilding.

Immediately following the floodwaters receding, the fire department turned its attention to aiding those affected by working closely with other emergency services and local authorities. They participated in comprehensive damage assessments that were crucial for securing timely relief. By systematically evaluating the extent of destruction across neighborhoods, the team identified areas of greatest need and prioritized resources where they were most urgently required. This meticulous approach to assessment not only facilitated access to immediate aid for countless families but also laid the groundwork for long-term rebuilding projects that would come to define the community's resilience.

The fire department's contributions did not end with these evaluations; they were deeply involved in coordinating community recovery initiatives aimed at restoring normalcy to everyday life. Through organizing distribution points for essential supplies and facilitating temporary housing solutions, they ensured that affected residents received the critical support they needed. Regular community meetings were held to update residents on recovery progress and listen to concerns, fostering a spirit of collaboration between the department and the community. This proactive engagement allowed them to tailor their support strategies to the unique needs and evolving challenges of the different neighborhoods they served.

An important aspect of the department's effectiveness in this recovery phase was their ability to form strong, sustained partnerships with various local organizations. By working alongside non-profits, faith-based groups, and local businesses, the department harnessed a wealth of resources and expertise to address the multifaceted needs of the community. These partnerships resulted in diverse support mechanisms, ranging from mental health counseling to employment services for displaced workers, which were integral to addressing the holistic well-being of the community. Such collaboration highlighted the department's commitment to a comprehensive approach to emergency management—one that recognized recovery extends beyond just physical reconstruction to include social and emotional rehabilitation.

Moreover, the fire department's collaborative spirit extended to forging alliances with regional and national bodies dedicated to disaster recovery. The integration of broader networks enabled them to bring in outside assistance, including federal disaster funds and volunteer workforces, which significantly bolstered local recovery efforts. By leveraging these larger resources, the department amplified Balch Springs' capacity to rebuild and recover, demonstrating a forward-thinking approach that transcended traditional emergency response roles.

Throughout this recovery period, a palpable shift occurred within the community—a transformation underscored by improved resilience and a sense of preparedness for future adversities. The collaborative efforts spearheaded by the fire department ensured that the community emerged stronger than before, fortified by new infrastructure and revitalized social fabric. Residents who had once been mere recipients of aid now found themselves empowered to actively contribute to rebuilding efforts, thus fostering a more robust and interconnected community environment.

Looking forward, the lessons learned from these experiences have become invaluable components of the department's ongoing mission to fortify community preparedness. Creating guidelines for future disaster response and recovery efforts became part of their legacy, encapsulating the principles of swift coordination, effective communication, and unwavering commitment to collective well-being. While the flood posed significant challenges, it also prompted the realization that preparedness and resilience are achievable through unity, shared purpose, and an unyielding focus on both immediate actions and long-term recovery goals.

Concluding Thoughts

Throughout the historic flood of 2022, the resilience and adaptability demonstrated by Chief Neal and his firefighting team in Balch Springs illuminated the essence of effective disaster response. Faced with unprecedented challenges, they not only adapted their skills in response to the dynamic floodwaters but also fostered seamless collaboration among various agencies. This comprehensive approach highlighted their readiness to confront diverse emergencies, underscoring the importance of interagency partnerships and diversified skill sets in crisis management. By efficiently utilizing specialized equipment and strategic planning, the team ensured safe evacuations and minimized risk, showcasing their commitment and preparedness in safeguarding the community.

The aftermath revealed a dedicated focus on recovery efforts, extending beyond immediate rescue operations. The fire department played a pivotal role in coordinating community-led initiatives, ensuring resources reached those most in need and fostering strong partnerships with local and national organizations. Through these efforts, the department facilitated a transformative recovery process, enhancing community resilience and preparedness for future adversities. As Balch Springs emerged stronger, this experience emphasized the value of unity, proactive planning, and continuous improvement in emergency response strategies. The lessons learned from this chapter serve as a guiding beacon for addressing not only the physical reconstruction but also the emotional and social rehabilitation necessary for holistic recovery.

Chapter 13: Crisis Management

Lessons from the Balch Springs Fires

Crisis management is a crucial skill for any community, particularly when faced with the unpredictable nature of disasters. This chapter dives into the heart of crisis management by examining the real-world example provided by the Balch Springs fires. The story begins with the fire outbreak and unfolds into a narrative that highlights the robustness and readiness of the Balch Springs community. By working in unison and forming strong alliances among its members, this community was able to tackle the catastrophic event head-on, demonstrating an exemplary model of crisis response. It wasn't just the flames that tested their resilience but also the requirement for seamless collaboration between residents and first responders, showcasing effective team dynamics under duress.

As we explore what transpired during the fires, readers will gain insights into how individual efforts meshed with organized emergency response strategies. The chapter delves into various aspects of local participation, from immediate neighborly assistance to the strategic involvement of volunteer groups and law enforcement. Beyond citizen engagement, it provides a window into the partnerships forged between local agencies and organizations which became pivotal in managing not only the immediate chaos but also orchestrating long-term recovery efforts. Readers will also learn about the contributions of different municipal departments in maintaining infrastructure, enabling the safe return of residents. This comprehensive examination reveals how pre-existing networks and collaborative spirit were harnessed effectively, offering valuable lessons to communities aiming to enhance their own crisis management capabilities. Through Balch Springs' story, we see how adversity can galvanize a community, reinforcing its ability to confront challenges with a united front.

Community Unity and Collaborative Efforts

As the fires raged through Balch Springs, a profound sense of unity emerged among residents, demonstrating the strength and resilience inherent in this community. This sense of cohesion was not spontaneous but rather a testament to the tight-knit nature of the area, where neighbors knew each other well enough to act swiftly in times of need. Stories abounded of individuals who went door-to-door, alerting families who might not have been aware of the impending danger. This immediate neighborly assistance became crucial in evacuating those most at risk, particularly the elderly and families with young children, ensuring their safety before emergency services arrived.

Beyond individual efforts, the collaboration with emergency responders played a pivotal role in managing the crisis effectively. Residents worked hand-in-hand with firefighters and police, providing local knowledge that was invaluable for strategically combating the blaze. This cooperation extended to organized volunteer groups who assisted in logistics such as traffic control, enabling the swift movement of emergency vehicles. The seamless interaction between residents and responders highlighted how pre-existing relationships and mutual trust can dramatically improve the efficiency and effectiveness of crisis management efforts.

The involvement of local organizations and agencies further emphasized the importance of established networks during crises. Community centers opened their doors to provide temporary shelter and coordinated with food banks to ensure evacuees had access to necessities. Churches and local businesses contributed by organizing donation drives and offering spaces for coordination meetings where plans were formulated and updated regularly. This concerted effort showcased how structured collaborations can harness the strengths of different entities, creating a tapestry of support that is more robust than any single element could achieve alone.

Particularly noteworthy was the role of law enforcement, medical services, and public works. These entities combined forces to provide a multifaceted response to the fires, each bringing unique expertise and resources. Law enforcement officials were instrumental in maintaining public order and ensuring evacuation orders were followed, which minimized chaos and confusion. Meanwhile, medical services were on standby to address health emergencies, from injuries sustained during evacuation to cases of smoke inhalation. Their readiness and prompt action were vital in preventing the escalation of a health crisis alongside the already daunting task of controlling the fire.

Public works departments also made significant contributions by clearing debris and ensuring roads remained accessible. Their work facilitated not only the movement of emergency services but also the eventual return of residents once the danger had passed. This foresight in maintaining infrastructure underscored the critical nature of having functional systems in place prior to a crisis, which can be rapidly adapted and deployed when needed.

To effectively manage future crises, it is essential to implement strategic guidelines that facilitate collaboration. By institutionalizing processes for joint training exercises between residents and emergency responders, communities can enhance their preparedness. Regular simulations and drills can foster a deeper understanding of roles, streamline communication channels, and create instinctual collaborative responses when real threats arise. Additionally, investing in community relationship-building activities would help cultivate trust and understanding, key components of an effective, unified response.

Aid Organizations and Learning from Adversity

In the unfolding chaos of the Balch Springs fires, aid organizations emerged as pivotal lifelines for those in crisis. Groups like the Red Cross and Sharing Life surged into action immediately, offering not just essential resources but hope to individuals who saw their lives disrupted. The presence of these organizations was a beacon of relief amid the turmoil, providing food, shelter, and medical supplies to those displaced by the infernos sweeping through their community. Their work exemplified the critical nature of immediate response during crises, ensuring that basic human needs were met promptly.

However, the impact of the Red Cross and Sharing Life extended far beyond the provision of immediate aid. They recognized the necessity of long-term recovery and support, working tirelessly even after the flames had been extinguished. These organizations understood that rebuilding lives is an ongoing process and that communities require sustained assistance to truly recover. Programs focused on mental health support, financial counselling, and housing rehabilitation were designed to help residents navigate the challenging path toward normalcy. By addressing both immediate and continuing needs, these groups demonstrated the importance of a comprehensive approach in crisis management.

Furthermore, their efforts served as a potent reminder of the significance of prolonged engagement in rebuilding efforts. In times of crisis, short-term solutions can only provide temporary relief; it's the enduring commitment to recovery that ultimately enables communities to heal and prosper once more. This dedication underscored the vital role such organizations play in facilitating resilience and adaptation, allowing individuals to rebuild not just their homes, but their lives.

In addition to the invaluable work of non-profits and aid organizations, the Fire Department's post-crisis reviews emerged as another crucial element of the Balch Springs response strategy. With meticulous assessments, they sought to learn from the recent events and identify areas for improvement. Through detailed analysis of what transpired, including response times, resource allocation, and communication effectiveness, they uncovered lessons that could drive future enhancements in crisis management techniques. Emphasizing continuous learning ensured that the fire department could evolve its strategies and adapt rapidly to any similar situations in the future.

These structured evaluations led to strategic innovations and procedural changes aimed at bolstering preparedness and response. By integrating technology, enhancing training programs, and refining coordination among various agencies, the lessons learned from these reviews fostered a culture of innovation and adaptability. Their focus on adaptive measures illustrated the value of flexibility in strengthening emergency response frameworks.

The community's ability to reflect on past experiences also played a vital role in fortifying its defenses against future challenges. This introspection wasn't just limited to institutional entities but was embraced by the residents themselves. Understanding the vulnerabilities exposed by the fires prompted a community-wide reevaluation of practices and preparedness measures, leading to stronger bonds and networks that reinforced communal support systems. Residents became more attuned to emergency protocols, fostering a shared responsibility for safety and wellbeing.

This collective sense of ownership was instrumental in reinforcing resilience, equipping Balch Springs with enhanced capabilities to withstand crises. As the community learned from its trials, it honed its adaptability—not merely to survive, but to thrive amidst uncertainty. The fires became a catalyst for transformation, embedding a resilient mindset within every layer of society.

Lessons Learned

The chapter illuminated how the Balch Springs community exemplified effective crisis management through unity and collaboration. From initial neighborly assistance to the coordination with emergency responders, the efforts demonstrated a deep-rooted culture of cooperation. Residents offered invaluable local knowledge to firefighters and police, enhancing strategic response efforts. Volunteer groups played vital roles in logistical support, showcasing how pre-existing relationships and trust accelerated crisis response efficiency. The chapter also highlighted the contributions of various local organizations, such as community centers and churches, that provided shelter and resources, illustrating the power of structured collaborations.

Furthermore, the examination of aid organizations like the Red Cross and Sharing Life revealed the critical importance of both immediate and long-term support during crises. These organizations not only responded swiftly to meet basic needs but also committed to ongoing recovery efforts, underscoring the significance of sustained engagement in rebuilding lives. The Fire Department's post-crisis evaluations offered valuable lessons, paving the way for future improvements in crisis management. Through this comprehensive exploration, the chapter demonstrates how unity, preparedness, and continuous learning are essential components in building robust defenses against adversity, fostering resilience within communities.

Chapter 14: Community Outreach and Fire Prevention Initiatives

The Essence of Community Risk Reduction

Community outreach and fire prevention initiatives form the backbone of effective community risk reduction strategies. These efforts are vital in bridging gaps between fire departments and the diverse populations they serve. Through proactive engagement, fire departments aim to foster trust and collaboration with residents, ensuring that safety measures are understood and accessible to all. By becoming an integral part of the community's fabric, firefighters can break down barriers and reduce the perception of their presence as solely reactive. This chapter delves into how these partnerships not only enhance immediate responses during emergencies but also cultivate a shared commitment to long-term safety goals.

The chapter explores various strategies employed by fire departments to engage communities in meaningful ways. It highlights innovative methods such as community events, educational programs for both children and adults, and the use of technology for wider reach and impact. The importance of cultural sensitivity is underscored, showing how tailoring outreach efforts to meet the unique needs of different groups can significantly boost participation and effectiveness. Furthermore, the chapter discusses the benefits of forming alliances with local businesses and organizations, illustrating how these collaborations fortify fire prevention campaigns and expand their scope. Readers will gain insights into how simple actions, like attending local gatherings or offering free smoke alarm installations, can pivotally shift perceptions and reinforce the role of fire departments as trusted allies committed to the well-being of the community.

Building Bridges with the Community

In community outreach and fire prevention initiatives, building trust and engagement between the fire department and the local population is a fundamental step. One effective strategy to achieve this is through emphasizing visibility and accessibility. Firefighters can often be seen as distant figures, only appearing when called upon. By participating in local events and informal interactions, such as community fairs or school activities, the fire department can become a familiar and friendly presence in the neighborhood. Attending these events not only allows firefighters to educate the public about fire safety but also to interact with residents on a personal level. This approach helps dismantle any perceived barriers, making it easy for community members to reach out for advice or assistance.

Engaging directly with residents goes beyond just attending events; it involves actively organizing activities that provide support and guidance. For instance, hosting open houses at fire stations where families can tour the facilities and meet the firefighting crew can demystify the services they provide. These visits offer opportunities for informal conversations where questions can be answered, and safety tips shared. Additionally, collaborating with local schools to conduct fire drills and safety audits instills a proactive mindset in young minds, fostering long-term understanding and preparedness. These interactions are crucial for reinforcing the idea that the fire department is a trusted ally invested in their community's well-being.

Understanding and respecting cultural diversity within the community is another integral aspect of successful engagement. Prioritizing cultural sensitivity and inclusivity ensures that all populations, regardless of their background, feel heard and valued. Recognizing cultural norms and language preferences enables the fire department to tailor their communication and educational efforts effectively. For example, offering safety materials in multiple languages and acknowledging cultural practices related to fire and cooking rituals can significantly enhance engagement with diverse groups. Furthermore, employing bilingual personnel or cultural liaisons can bridge communication gaps, facilitating more meaningful dialogue and collaboration.

Demonstrating genuine care and investment in community well-being naturally leads to trusted partnerships. When the fire department consistently shows commitment to residents' safety, trust is built over time. Establishing programs, such as free smoke alarm installations or first aid training sessions, underscores this dedication. By offering tangible help, the department showcases its role not merely as an emergency responder but as an active contributor to community resilience. Engaging in joint projects with local organizations further solidifies these relationships, creating a network of allies all working towards the common goal of reducing risks and enhancing safety.

The success of these initiatives depends largely on the consistent and open communication between the fire department and the community. Inviting feedback from residents on how best to address their needs can guide the implementation of various programs, ensuring that they are relevant and effective. Regular surveys or town hall meetings provide a platform for citizens to voice their concerns and contribute ideas, fostering a sense of shared responsibility. Listening to the community helps the fire department to adapt its strategies, accordingly, showing responsiveness and flexibility in addressing emerging challenges.

Moreover, maintaining a visible presence within the community fosters a sense of reassurance among residents. When people frequently see firefighters in non-emergency situations, it reinforces the perception that the fire department is readily available and willing to assist. Simple gestures, like firefighters visiting schools to read stories or participate in local charity events, can have a lasting impact. These actions humanize the department, showcasing firefighters as approachable neighbors rather than distant authorities.

To deepen connections, the fire department should also engage with key community leaders and influencers who can advocate for fire safety initiatives within their circles. Collaborating with religious leaders, educators, and local government officials can extend the department's reach and amplify its message. These leaders often hold significant sway and can help rally their communities behind shared safety goals. Building a coalition of support around fire prevention can lead to broader buy-in and participation from the public.

Innovative Fire Prevention Education and Collaboration

Developing fire prevention programs that cater to the specific needs of a community is a crucial element in reducing risk and enhancing safety. One of the first steps in this process is implementing educational initiatives aimed at children. Conducting age-appropriate workshops in schools enables educators to teach children the fundamentals of fire safety, which can significantly impact their understanding and response to potential hazards. These workshops might involve interactive sessions where children learn how to safely evacuate during a fire or the importance of not playing with matches and lighters. By using engaging methods such as role-playing, games, and demonstrations, these lessons are more likely to leave a lasting impression on young minds.

Furthermore, addressing fire prevention with adults calls for a different approach. Organizing seminars and workshops tailored to adult audiences is essential for imparting knowledge about home fire prevention and emergency planning. These gatherings can serve as platforms for discussing practical measures like installing smoke alarms, creating family emergency plans, and maintaining clear escape routes. Participants could engage in hands-on activities, such as practicing the use of fire extinguishers or running through evacuation drills. Through open discussions and expert-led sessions, adults can gain a comprehensive understanding of how to protect their homes and families from potential fire risks.

In today's digital age, leveraging technology to share fire safety information provides an innovative avenue for outreach. Digital tools, such as social media, webinars, and mobile apps, offer unique opportunities for disseminating vital information quickly and effectively. A community fire department might utilize social media platforms to share regular updates, tips, and instructional videos on various aspects of fire safety. Interactive webinars can allow residents to interact with fire prevention experts, ask questions, and receive real-time guidance. Additionally, developing user-friendly apps equipped with features like emergency alerts and step-by-step guides for fire preparedness can empower individuals to take proactive measures in safeguarding their environments.

Creating effective fire prevention strategies also involves fostering cooperative partnerships within the community. Collaborating with local businesses and organizations can amplify efforts and encourage shared responsibility in minimizing fire risks. For instance, partnerships with hardware stores might facilitate discounted rates for fire safety equipment, such as smoke detectors and fire extinguishers, making them more accessible to residents. Engaging with insurance companies could lead to informative sessions on the financial implications of fire damage and the benefits of preventive measures. Furthermore, working alongside community centers or local non-profits can help tailor fire safety campaigns to address specific needs, ensuring that diverse populations are adequately informed and protected.

An important consideration when designing these programs is targeting outreach to vulnerable populations. Certain groups, such as the elderly, low-income families, or non-native speakers, may face unique challenges in accessing fire safety resources. Therefore, it is vital to develop guidelines that ensure these populations are reached effectively. This might involve organizing bilingual workshops, providing free or subsidized safety equipment, or collaborating with local agencies to facilitate transportation to events. Tailoring efforts to meet the needs of these groups helps bridge gaps and promotes inclusivity, ensuring that no one is left unprotected.

Moreover, adopting innovative technologies in outreach efforts can greatly enhance communication and engagement. Utilizing virtual reality (VR) simulations, for instance, can provide realistic and immersive fire safety training experiences. Residents could participate in simulated fire scenarios, learning firsthand how to react in emergencies without facing actual danger. Virtual tours of escape routes or interactive tutorials on utilizing fire extinguishers can also be highly effective. By integrating cutting-edge technology into outreach initiatives, fire departments can attract wider attention and interest, particularly among tech-savvy individuals, thereby reinforcing key prevention messages.

While engaging with digital and technological tools has its merits, nothing replaces human connection in building trust and commitment within the community. However, establishing collaborative partnerships with local businesses and organizations can further reinforce these efforts. By tapping into existing networks and resources, fire departments can leverage the strengths of different entities to bolster fire prevention campaigns. Though direct guidelines may not be necessary here, highlighting successful case studies of partnerships can illustrate the significant impact that collaboration can achieve. Witnessing tangible results from combined efforts underscores the community's collective power in mitigating fire risks.

Lastly, incorporating routine home inspections as part of fire prevention strategies plays a critical role in identifying potential hazards before they escalate into emergencies. Guidelines for these inspections can include recommended steps and checks, such as examining electrical wiring for faults, ensuring flammable materials are stored safely, and confirming that smoke detectors are functioning correctly. Implementing regular inspection services allows trained professionals to pinpoint issues and provide actionable advice, empowering residents to maintain safer living environments. Encouraging homeowners to adopt these practices can substantially decrease the likelihood of fire incidents while fostering a culture of vigilance and preparedness.

Bringing It All Together

Throughout this chapter, we've explored the vital strategies that enhance community safety through proactive engagement and fire prevention. The emphasis has been on building bridges between the fire department and the diverse communities they serve. By making firefighters more visible and accessible at local events and through informal interactions, these steps dismantle barriers and foster a sense of trust. Programs like open houses at fire stations and collaborations with schools enable meaningful exchanges and promote a deeper understanding of fire safety. Cultural sensitivity has been highlighted as crucial for effective communication with diverse populations, ensuring inclusivity and accessibility in fire prevention efforts.

Partnering with community leaders extends the reach of fire safety initiatives and amplifies their impact. Collaborating with key figures like religious leaders or educator's aids in garnering community support and participation. Strategies have also included fostering cooperative partnerships with local businesses and organizations, creating a network dedicated to reducing risks. Digital tools and innovative technologies further expand outreach possibilities, making information readily available and engaging. Maintaining a human connection underpins all efforts, underscoring the fire department's role not only as an emergency responder but as a dedicated community ally committed to safeguarding residents' safety and well-being.

Chapter 15: Mutual Aid Cooperation

A Friendly Partnership for Safety

Navigating interagency cooperation and mutual aid is fundamental to enhancing community safety and building more resilient societies. The collaboration between various agencies can significantly improve emergency response capabilities, ensuring that crises are managed efficiently and effectively. Establishing strong partnerships among law enforcement, fire departments, emergency medical services, and other relevant entities forms the core of these collaborative efforts. Each agency brings unique strengths and resources, which, when combined, create a robust network capable of addressing complex emergencies. These interagency relationships not only enhance operational readiness but also foster a sense of shared responsibility toward community safety.

In this chapter, the reader will explore the dynamics of interagency cooperation and how mutual and automatic aid agreements play a critical role in reinforcing emergency responses. We examine the importance of regular meetings, joint training exercises, and informal interactions that lay the foundation for effective teamwork among diverse organizations. Additionally, the significance of trust and transparency in maintaining these collaborations will be highlighted, demonstrating how agencies can work together to optimize resource utilization and minimize chaos during incidents. Furthermore, the chapter delves into structured planning through formal agreements and after-action reviews, providing insights into how these strategies contribute to continuous improvement and preparedness for future challenges.

Fostering Friendly Relationships and Shared Commitments

Building robust interagency relationships forms the backbone of effective emergency responses. Agencies, working together, can ensure swift and efficient handling of crises by leveraging each other's strengths. A key aspect of this collaboration is regular meetings and discussions, which provide platforms for sharing best practices and coordinating efforts. These sessions enable agencies to stay updated on developments across sectors and learn from experiences, setting a foundation for improved coordination.

Attend these meetings; agency representatives discuss strategies, address challenges, and explore opportunities for joint operations. For instance, local health departments might share insights with school systems on managing public health emergencies, leading to better preparedness in educational institutions (Shoaf et al., 2014). Such interactions create an environment where agencies, comfortable sharing their methods, contribute to a cohesive response network. Through these conversations, agencies can establish a unified approach to tackling emergencies.

Joint training exercises are another crucial element in fostering strong interagency relationships. By engaging in simulated scenarios, teams from different organizations can improve interoperability and understand each other's procedures. This hands-on experience is invaluable as it highlights potential gaps in plans and helps refine protocols for future incidents. For example, when fire departments train alongside emergency medical services, they gain insights into each other's workflows and enhance their ability to work seamlessly during real emergencies. The importance of these exercises cannot be overstated, as they lay the groundwork for cooperation that saves lives.

Moreover, informal interactions play a significant role in breaking down barriers between personnel from various organizations. Social gatherings, team-building activities, or simply casual conversations during breaks help build camaraderie and unity. These moments of connection go beyond professional boundaries and foster personal bonds that translate into effective teamwork during crises. When individuals know and trust each other personally, they're more likely to collaborate efficiently, communicate openly, and support one another, especially during high-stress situations.

Collaboration with law enforcement is pivotal in ensuring seamless integration of efforts to address public safety challenges. Police, fire departments, and emergency services often work hand-in-hand during incidents, requiring a clear understanding of each other's roles. Regular coordination meetings between these entities help clarify responsibilities, streamline communication channels, and develop joint strategies for various emergencies. By fostering such alliances, communities benefit from well-coordinated responses that minimize chaos and maximize resource utilization.

The development and maintenance of mutual trust among agencies underpin all these collaborative efforts. Trust is built through transparency, consistent communication, and keeping promises. Agencies must demonstrate reliability in their commitments, fostering assurance that they will act in concert when needed. As such, fostering trust should be a continuous endeavor, nurtured through sustained interagency interactions and shared successes.

Having recognized the need for structured planning, agencies can also establish formal agreements, like memorandums of understanding or joint operating agreements. These documents outline expectations, roles, and responsibilities, providing a legal framework for collaboration. They serve not only as reminders of commitments but also protect partners' interests during complex operations. Written agreements facilitate smoother cooperation by clearly defining boundaries and preventing misunderstandings.

Furthermore, after-action reviews are essential components of ongoing improvement in interagency cooperation. Post-incident evaluations allow agencies to reflect on their performance, identify areas for enhancement, and develop actionable insights for future scenarios (2014). Conducting these reviews collaboratively ensures diverse perspectives are considered, enriching the learning process. Agencies can then refine their practices based on collective input, ensuring stronger preparedness for upcoming challenges.

Mutual and Automatic Aid Agreements: Enhancing Emergency Response

In the ever-evolving landscape of emergency response, mutual and automatic aid agreements emerge as pivotal tools that enhance the capacity of agencies to respond swiftly and effectively to emergencies. Mutual aid agreements are foundational in this context, acting as formal arrangements between neighboring fire departments or emergency services that ensure additional resources can be dispatched upon request during large-scale emergencies. The essence of mutual aid lies in its ability to strengthen community resilience by supplementing local resources with external support when needed most. This collaboration becomes crucial in situations where a single department's resources may be stretched thin, such as natural disasters or major accidents.

Automatic aid agreements go a step further by setting predefined criteria under which aid can be mobilized instantaneously. Unlike mutual aid, which requires a formal request once an incident occurs, automatic aid operates on a proactive basis, pre-arranging assistance that is automatically triggered by specific situations. For instance, if a particular type of emergency occurs that surpasses local capabilities—as defined by the agreement—neighboring agencies are immediately notified to provide necessary support. Such arrangements not only expedite response times but also streamline coordination, ensuring that communities receive timely intervention without the administrative delays associated with ad-hoc requests.

The effectiveness of these agreements extends beyond mere operational enhancement. One significant benefit is their contribution to lowering homeowners' insurance rates. Insurance providers often assess the capabilities of local fire departments and emergency services when determining policy rates—regions with robust mutual and automatic aid frameworks demonstrate higher efficiency and effectiveness in handling incidents. This leads to reduced risk assessments, translating into lower premiums for residents within those jurisdictions. Such financial incentives serve as a tangible testament to the value of interagency cooperation, offering communal benefits that reach every homeowner.

Moreover, partnerships with state and federal entities further amplify the impact of mutual and automatic aid agreements. These partnerships facilitate access to additional resources, expertise, and funding, providing localized efforts with a broader range of tools to effectively manage emergencies. Collaboration at the state and federal levels brings a wealth of knowledge and specialized equipment that may not be otherwise available to individual departments. Federal grants and training programs become accessible, enabling local agencies to enhance their operational readiness. This partnership model underscores the importance of multi-tiered support systems, where each level of government plays a role in fortifying community safety nets.

To ensure the success of mutual and automatic aid agreements, initiating regular meetings and collaborative discussions among participating agencies is imperative. These forums enable departments to exchange best practices, address potential challenges, and update protocols to align with emerging threats or technological advancements. Through dialogue, agencies can fine-tune their agreements, ensuring that both operational demands and community needs are met efficiently.

Opportunities for joint training exercises and drills also play a critical role in optimizing these cooperative frameworks. By engaging in joint simulations, agencies improve interoperability and understanding of one another's procedures. This practical approach allows personnel from different organizations to work together seamlessly during actual emergencies, reducing friction and enhancing overall response quality. Training drills also serve as testing grounds for refining automatic aid criteria, ensuring that triggers are relevant and effective.

Concluding Thoughts

The chapter has delved into the collaboration between agencies, focusing on how these partnerships enhance community safety. Through open communication and the sharing of experiences, agencies can address challenges together, leveraging each other's strengths to manage emergencies efficiently. Regular meetings and joint training exercises are crucial in this process, as they allow agencies to understand one another's procedures and work towards seamless coordination during crises. Such interactions foster a unified approach, ensuring that public safety is addressed with agility and precision.

Additionally, formal agreements like mutual and automatic aid provide a framework for structured collaboration, which is vital in large-scale emergencies. These agreements not only bolster resource availability but also improve response times by establishing predefined protocols. Partnerships with state and federal entities further reinforce local efforts, bringing expertise and resources that individual agencies might lack. By maintaining trust and commitment, these collaborative frameworks significantly enhance community resilience, underscoring the shared responsibility in safeguarding public well-being.

Chapter 16: Mentoring and Leadership

Development within the Department

Mentoring and leadership development within the department are foundational components that significantly contribute to the growth and cohesion of firefighters. These aspects serve as lifelines, fostering a culture where knowledge and skills are passed seamlessly from seasoned veterans to eager newcomers. Mentorship is not merely an activity; it is a critical engagement that empowers individuals by connecting them with experienced mentors who provide guidance, share invaluable insights, and instill core professional values. In a field where every decision can have life-altering consequences, having access to a mentor transforms a firefighter's journey, blending learning with practical experience in a way that enhances both personal and collective capabilities. This chapter delves into how these relationships shape not only the technical expertise of individuals but also their leadership potential.

We will explore the intricate dynamics of mentorship, examining its impact on skill transfer, teamwork, and personal development. The narrative will take readers through the processes involved in effective mentoring, highlighting how these engagements foster confidence and prepare firefighters for real-world challenges. Furthermore, we will delve into the role of formal and informal mentoring programs, seeing how they collectively contribute to nurturing leadership qualities. Leadership development initiatives, structured within the department, offer strategic support that aligns with mentoring efforts, encouraging inclusivity and bridging gaps between various levels within the hierarchy. These programs often include workshops, seminars, and collaborative projects, each designed to cultivate leadership skills while promoting a culture of continuous self-improvement. By understanding these frameworks, readers can appreciate how mentoring and leadership development bolster departmental success and individual fulfillment, ultimately shaping a more cohesive and resilient firefighting community.

The Role of Mentorship in Professional Growth

Mentorship is a cornerstone in the professional development of firefighters, serving to bridge the knowledge gap between seasoned professionals and newcomers. This form of guidance creates an invaluable platform where experienced firefighters are able to impart their acquired wisdom, skills, and technical expertise to junior members. Such skill transfer not only ensures that critical information is retained within the department but also prepares younger firefighters to tackle the challenges they will face throughout their careers. As mentors share real-world experiences, they provide practical insights that go beyond textbook learning, making the learning experience richer and more applicable to everyday scenarios.

Firefighting, by its very nature, demands teamwork and a deep understanding of various techniques and procedures. Therefore, mentorship plays a pivotal role in ensuring that these essential skills are effectively passed down. Through one-on-one interactions, apprentices gain hands-on experiences that reinforce their training and help them build confidence in their abilities. Additionally, mentees have the chance to ask questions and learn from the direct experiences of their more knowledgeable counterparts, fostering an environment where curiosity is encouraged and learning is constant.

Beyond the transfer of technical skills, mentorship serves as a crucial tool for instilling core values and leadership qualities in future leaders. Often, young firefighters look up to their mentors not just for guidance in emergencies but also for their steadfast commitment to duty and ethical conduct. Mentors serve as role models, demonstrating not only the importance of expertise but also the value of integrity, teamwork, and resilience. Such personal attributes are vital in cultivating a strong sense of camaraderie within teams, creating bonds that enhance cooperation and boost morale.

The nurturing of leadership qualities within a mentorship framework can transform how individuals perceive and approach their roles. By observing their mentors' decision-making processes and leadership styles, junior firefighters can begin to develop their own approaches to leadership. This exposure provides them with diverse strategies for handling stress, making quick yet informed decisions, and motivating others, all of which are crucial skills for any aspiring leader.

Departmental leadership programs play a strategic role in supporting this mentoring process by offering structured opportunities for growth. These programs often include workshops, seminars, and collaborative projects designed to foster leadership capabilities while promoting inclusivity. Such initiatives enable participants from various backgrounds to contribute unique perspectives and insights, enriching the learning experience. Inclusivity within these programs ensures that every firefighter, regardless of their cultural or personal background, feels valued and empowered to pursue advanced roles.

While the primary goal of these programs might be leadership development, they simultaneously bring about personal growth and enhanced self-awareness among participants. Firefighters are encouraged to assess their strengths and weaknesses critically, paving the way for continuous self-improvement. Furthermore, inclusive programs can lead to greater innovation, as diverse teams work together to find creative solutions to common challenges faced by the department.

To sum up, mentorship within the firefighter community is instrumental in both skill transfer and the nurturing of leadership capacities. It offers a reliable means for conveying essential knowledge and honing technical competencies that must remain within the department's toolkit. At the same time, mentorship shapes personal development by introducing mentees to values and practices that define effective leaders. The interaction between mentor and mentee fosters an enriching relationship built on trust and mutual respect, laying the foundation for stronger teams and better-prepared individuals.

Guidelines for developing successful mentorship programs emphasize the need for a tailored approach, adjusting to the unique demands of firefighting as a profession. It is crucial to match mentors and mentees based on compatibility to maximize the benefits of the relationship. Clear communication pathways should be established, ensuring feedback is constructive and goal-oriented. Regular evaluation of program outcomes can ascertain whether objectives are being met and guide necessary adjustments to improve effectiveness.

Instilling values and leadership qualities through mentorship requires intentionality and careful planning. Departments should encourage a culture of openness where mentees feel comfortable seeking advice and sharing their thoughts. Formal mentorship meetings supplemented by informal interactions can deepen the mentor-mentee bond, providing additional learning opportunities outside structured sessions.

Leadership Development and Inclusive Culture

In the world of firefighting, where every second counts and teamwork is essential, leadership development plays a crucial role in shaping both personal and departmental advancements. One of the cornerstones of this advancement is fostering an environment where leadership opportunities are accessible to all, regardless of rank. This approach not only strengthens the department as a whole but also empowers individual firefighters to rise through the ranks with confidence and competence.

Fire departments have increasingly focused on breaking down barriers that traditionally restricted access to leadership training and mentorship. Open access to leadership development initiatives means that every firefighter, from the newest recruit to the seasoned veteran, has the opportunity to enhance their skills and contribute more effectively to the team. By creating pathways for learning and growth, departments not only equip individuals with the necessary tools to handle crisis situations but also encourage innovation and adaptability.

A prime example of this approach is the implementation of informal mentoring programs within the department. These programs provide a platform for experienced firefighters to share insights and knowledge in a less formal setting, facilitating a free exchange of ideas. Informal mentoring encourages relationships built on trust and respect, which can lead to new perspectives and fresh approaches to solving problems. By engaging in these informal interactions, firefighters develop communication and leadership skills organically, making them more prepared for future roles.

Succession planning is another vital component in ensuring departmental continuity and stability. Identifying potential leaders early in their careers allows for targeted development, aligning individual career goals with departmental needs. This proactive approach ensures that when leadership transitions occur, they happen seamlessly, minimizing disruptions to operations and maintaining the morale of the team. A well-structured succession plan involves regular evaluations and feedback sessions, helping aspirants understand areas of improvement and providing them with a clear path to achieving leadership roles.

Emphasizing inclusivity within leadership initiatives fosters a culture of creativity and innovation. When team members from diverse backgrounds and experiences are encouraged to participate, they bring unique viewpoints and ideas to the table. This diversity is a powerful asset, enabling the department to devise more effective strategies and solutions. Encouraging women, minorities, and individuals from various socio-economic backgrounds to engage in leadership development ensures that the department mirrors the community it serves, strengthening its relationship with the public.

An inclusive approach also addresses and dismantles any existing biases or stereotypes, promoting fairness and equality. As firefighters embrace diversity, they learn to value different perspectives, enhancing collaboration and teamwork. Departments that prioritize inclusivity report higher rates of job satisfaction among personnel, as individuals feel valued and respected for their contributions.

Through these inclusive leadership initiatives, personal development becomes intrinsically linked with departmental success. Firefighters are motivated to push beyond their limits, driven by a sense of belonging and purpose. As they acquire new skills and experiences, they become advocates for change, inspiring peers and contributing to a positive organizational culture.

Furthermore, mentorship and leadership programs offer opportunities for firefighters to step out of their comfort zones. Workshops, seminars, and role-playing exercises simulate real-life scenarios, challenging participants to think critically and act decisively under pressure. These experiences build resilience and self-confidence, equipping individuals with the mental fortitude needed to tackle emergencies efficiently.

While structured programs are essential, the true spirit of leadership development thrives in everyday interactions. Leading by example and championing an open-door policy encourages transparency and constant communication between all levels of the department. Firefighters learn from observing senior officers who demonstrate integrity, empathy, and dedication. This hands-on learning experience reinforces the importance of ethical decision-making and accountability in leadership.

The journey of personal and departmental growth through inclusive leadership initiatives is not without its challenges. Resistance to change, ingrained habits, and resource constraints can pose obstacles; however, the commitment to fostering a supportive and empowering environment ultimately pays off. Departments that embrace these initiatives often witness improved morale, reduced turnover rates, and enhanced operational effectiveness.

Concluding Thoughts

Mentorship and leadership development within the fire department significantly impact both individual growth and the overall cohesion of the team. This chapter has explored how these practices bridge knowledge gaps, ensuring that critical skills and values are passed seamlessly from experienced firefighters to new recruits. By fostering environments where learning and curiosity thrive, mentorship cultivates confidence and competence in junior members. Simultaneously, leadership initiatives provide structured pathways for all firefighters to develop their potential, promoting inclusivity and allowing individuals to contribute effectively regardless of their background or rank.

The emphasis on mentorship and leadership is crucial not only for skill transfer but also for personal growth. As firefighters engage with mentors and participate in leadership programs, they develop vital attributes such as integrity, resilience, and teamwork. These qualities lay the foundation for effective leadership and create a sense of camaraderie within the department. Though challenges exist, such as resistance to change and resource limitations, a commitment to empowering individuals through mentorship ultimately strengthens the department. In embracing diversity and innovation, fire departments enhance their operational effectiveness while inspiring personal growth and motivation among their personnel.

Chapter 17: Maintaining Work and Life

Balance as a Fire Chief

Balancing work and personal life is a demanding challenge for many professionals, and this holds particularly true for those in leadership roles within high-stakes environments like firefighting. The role of a fire chief does not merely require operational oversight; it demands the ability to lead under pressure, often amidst life-or-death situations. As we delve into Chief Neal's strategies, we see a leader who not only recognizes the significance of maintaining equilibrium between professional duties and personal health but also implements thoughtful measures to ensure that both he and his team are equipped to achieve this balance. His approach serves as an inspiring example for others seeking to manage similar responsibilities while prioritizing well-being.

In this chapter, readers will explore Chief Neal's comprehensive strategies for nurturing work-life balance among his team. Through detailed insights, the chapter unveils how Neal has crafted a supportive environment that tackles mental and physical wellness head-on. Attention is given to practical measures, such as structured work hours and mental health support, which aim to mitigate stress and prevent burnout. The chapter also examines how Neal has fostered open communication within the department, encouraging a culture where team members feel valued and empowered to express their concerns. Readers will gain a deeper understanding of how these initiatives not only enhance individual well-being but also contribute to improved team performance and resilience. By highlighting the importance of personal pursuits alongside professional commitments, the chapter underscores the holistic philosophy that has become pivotal to Chief Neal's successful leadership style.

Strategies for Supporting Team Well-Being

Chief Neal's dedication to fostering holistic well-being among firefighters is exemplary, emphasizing the importance of maintaining work-life balance within the high-pressure environment of a fire department. His approach centers around the implementation of various initiatives designed to support both the mental and physical health of his team. The first step he took was regulating work hours to ensure that firefighters were not overexerting themselves. By establishing a structured schedule, Neal ensured that each member had ample time to recover from the demands of their job. This structure not only improved productivity but also reduced burnout, allowing firefighters to be at their best when responding to emergencies.

In addition to managing work hours, Chief Neal championed the integration of mental health resources as a fundamental aspect of supporting his team. Recognizing the emotional strain that firefighting entails, he instituted programs that offer counseling and stress management workshops. These resources provide firefighters with tools to handle trauma and maintain their mental resilience, ultimately contributing to a healthier workplace environment. By normalizing discussions about mental health, Neal created a culture where seeking help is seen as a strength rather than a weakness.

Another cornerstone of Neal's strategy was the establishment of open communication channels throughout the department. He understood that effective communication is critical in addressing the challenges faced by his team. Regular meetings and forums were organized to encourage firefighters to voice their concerns and share insights freely. These sessions allowed for an exchange of ideas and solutions, fostering an atmosphere where everyone felt heard and valued. Neal also set up a mentoring system, pairing seasoned firefighters with newer members to provide guidance and support. This mentorship not only benefited individual growth but strengthened the overall cohesion of the department.

A significant part of maintaining well-being within the team involved prioritizing camaraderie and mutual support. Chief Neal believed that a close-knit team would be more resilient in the face of adversity. To build this sense of unity, he organized team-building activities such as retreats and community service projects. These events allowed firefighters to bond outside of the usual high-stress scenarios, creating friendships that enhanced collaboration during emergencies. By promoting a culture of teamwork, Neal reinforced the idea that everyone could rely on each other, further bolstering their collective ability to overcome challenges.

Beyond professional responsibilities, Neal encouraged his team to engage in personal activities and hobbies as a means of finding fulfillment. Understanding that a balanced life extends beyond the workplace, he actively supported firefighters in pursuing interests that mattered to them personally. Whether it was participating in sports, music, or art, Neal emphasized the value of having outlets for creativity and relaxation. Such engagement in personal pursuits helped firefighters recharge mentally and physically, giving them a broader perspective on life and work.

A guideline worth mentioning here involves facilitating access to these personal activities. Chief Neal introduced flexible scheduling options, allowing firefighters to participate in community events, family gatherings, and personal celebrations without feeling guilty about taking time off. Furthermore, the department offered classes and workshops tailored to various interests, encouraging personal development alongside professional growth. This arrangement not only enriched the lives of the firefighters but also contributed positively to their performance when on duty.

Through these multifaceted strategies, Chief Neal successfully cultivated an environment that supports holistic well-being among his firefighters. His emphasis on regulated work hours and mental health resources laid a strong foundation for reducing stress and enhancing productivity. Open communication channels and team-building efforts fostered a supportive and cohesive community, ensuring that every firefighter felt a sense of belonging and trust. Finally, by valuing personal activities and interests outside of work, Neal demonstrated his commitment to a balanced life that respects both professional duties and personal happiness.

Balancing Leadership Challenges with Personal Life

As a Fire Chief, Neal is frequently confronted with the intricate task of maintaining balance amidst significant leadership responsibilities. One of his primary approaches in overcoming these challenges lies in gaining trust and respect from seasoned firefighters. This is no easy feat, especially while spearheading progressive changes within the department. Neal understands that change can be met with resistance, particularly when it alters long-standing practices. Therefore, he prioritizes open communication and transparency as his tools for building rapport. By actively listening to the concerns of his team and involving them in decision-making processes, Neal fosters an environment of collaboration and mutual respect. He recognizes that seasoned firefighters bring invaluable experience to the table, which is why their insights are integral to the successful implementation of new initiatives.

Neal's chosen path highlights how essential trust is in orchestrating change. For instance, when considering updating training protocols to include advanced technology and techniques, he engages veteran firefighters in meaningful discussions. By valuing their input, he not only bridges generational gaps but also encourages innovation. His ability to earn the trust of his team enables him to navigate the complexities of leadership with both confidence and humility, effectively turning skeptics into allies who champion departmental advancements.

In addition to fostering internal trust, collaboration with city leaders plays a pivotal role in Chief Neal's strategy. Working closely with municipal authorities often involves managing differing priorities and securing essential resources. Neal approaches these interactions with diplomacy and a clear understanding of the broader community context. Recognizing the varying demands placed upon city budgets and resources, he advocates for the needs of his department through well-researched proposals that underscore the benefits of robust firefighting capabilities.

His efforts to collaborate with city officials extend beyond budgetary discussions. Neal understands that forming strategic alliances with key stakeholders is instrumental in achieving departmental goals. Through consistent dialogue and relationship-building, he ensures that the fire department's priorities align with those of the community and its leadership. This alignment not only facilitates resource acquisition but also strengthens public trust in the department's mission. Neal's adeptness in this arena reflects his broader philosophy: teamwork extends beyond the confines of the firehouse, encompassing partnerships with all facets of local governance.

Central to Neal's leadership style is his perspective on obstacles—as opportunities for growth and transformation within a dynamic team. Instead of viewing challenges as impediments, he embraces them as catalysts for improvement. Neal cultivates a culture where setbacks are constructive learning experiences, encouraging team members to explore creative solutions. By nurturing resilience and adaptability among his firefighters, Neal equips the department with the ability to thrive in an ever-changing landscape.

A poignant example of this is Neal's handling of increased emergency call volumes in recent years. Rather than succumbing to pressure, he saw the situation as a chance to optimize response strategies. Engaging the team in problem-solving sessions, they collectively brainstormed ways to enhance efficiency without compromising safety. This approach empowered firefighters to take ownership of innovative ideas, boosting morale and demonstrating the value of adaptability in high-pressure environments.

Furthermore, Neal's commitment to personal well-being shines through his leadership actions. He understands that leading by example is powerful, and thus, he diligently maintains his own work-life balance amidst professional responsibilities. Neal practices self-care rituals, such as regular exercise and meditation, which he openly shares with his team. In doing so, he underscores the importance of mental health matters and encourages others to prioritize their well-being.

This demonstration of self-care serves as a model for his team, highlighting that maintaining a balanced life is not merely an individual necessity but a professional obligation. Neal's acknowledgment of the intrinsic link between personal health and job performance conveys a critical message: Firefighters must sustain their physical and mental capacities to serve the community effectively. By promoting a culture that values personal well-being, Neal ensures his team is resilient, focused, and prepared for the unique challenges of their profession.

Chief Neal's experiences provide valuable lessons in leadership and personal balance. Through trust-building within his department, strategic collaborations with city leaders, and a forward-thinking approach to challenges, he exemplifies the essence of effective leadership. Moreover, by modeling commitment to personal well-being, Neal inspires his team to embrace self-care as an integral component of their role.

Concluding Thoughts

In exploring Chief Neal's strategies, we find a thoughtful balance between managing the demanding role of fire chief and nurturing both personal well-being and team support. Neal's approach emphasizes structured work hours and mental health resources, which form a robust framework for reducing stress among firefighters. These efforts are complemented by open communication channels that foster trust and unity within the department. His attention to building camaraderie and encouraging personal interests outside work underscores his commitment to a holistic approach to well-being. By cultivating an environment where every firefighter feels valued and supported, Neal ensures a resilient and collaborative team ready to face any challenge.

Chief Neal extends his leadership beyond the firehouse walls, seamlessly integrating his department's priorities with those of city leaders through strategic collaborations. His ability to transform obstacles into opportunities highlights his innovative approach to leadership. Neal's dedication to personal well-being serves as a powerful model for his team, demonstrating the importance of self-care in maintaining peak professional performance. Through his actions, he inspires his firefighters to view personal health as essential to their roles, ensuring they remain focused and prepared. His leadership offers valuable lessons on balancing responsibilities while fostering a culture of resilience and innovation.

Chapter 18: Policy and Procedural

Adjustments for Efficiency

The efficiency and effectiveness of any fire department hinge on well-structured policies and procedures. In the Balch Springs Fire Department, Chief Neal's strategic adjustments have significantly improved the operations and capabilities of the team. By revisiting established protocols and introducing new technologies, the department has revolutionized resource management and emergency response strategies. Chief Neal's leadership style emphasizes adaptability and innovation in facing the evolving challenges within the community. His commitment to operational excellence ensures that the department is not only prepared for current demands but also agile enough to tackle future obstacles.

This chapter delves into the specific policy and procedural changes initiated under Chief Neal's guidance, illustrating their profound impact on the department's functionality. From the integration of advanced systems like Computer-Aided Dispatch (CAD) to the implementation of sophisticated training programs, each initiative is explored in detail. Readers will gain insight into how these technological advancements and updated practices significantly reduced emergency response times and enhanced the department's overall preparedness. Furthermore, the chapter highlights the role of comprehensive policy manuals in standardizing operations and fostering a culture of accountability among personnel. Through these discussions, the narrative illuminates the transformative journey of the Balch Springs Fire Department toward becoming a model of efficiency and responsiveness.

Streamlining Operations and Enhancing Training

The quest for improved efficiency within the Balch Springs Fire Department has been guided by Chief Neal's strategic approach to policy and procedural adjustments. Central to this endeavor is the integration of technology, which has revolutionized how resources are deployed, and emergencies are managed. One significant stride in this direction was the introduction of a Computer-Aided Dispatch (CAD) system. This technological advancement transformed the way calls were managed, leading to a more agile allocation of resources. Prior to CAD, dispatchers relied heavily on manual processes that consumed precious time during emergencies. With CAD's implementation, the department witnessed a noticeable reduction in response times. The CAD system streamlined communication between dispatchers and responders, allowing for quicker mobilization of firefighting units and ensuring that the right resources reached the incident scene without delay.

Beyond improving emergency response times, the CAD system also equipped the department with valuable data analytics capabilities. By analyzing patterns from previous incidents, the department could anticipate resource needs better and allocate them more efficiently. This proactive approach not only enhanced immediate response capabilities but also contributed to long-term strategic planning. In addition, CAD systems often come with mapping features that provide real-time updates on road conditions and traffic patterns, assisting in choosing the most efficient routes for deploying fire units, further cutting down on response times.

Further enhancing operational efficiency, updated incident command systems have played a pivotal role in coordinating responses and optimizing resource usage during critical situations. These systems established clear lines of communication and command among different teams, fostering more organized and coordinated efforts during emergencies. Prior to these updates, there was often confusion and overlap between units responding to the same incident. By employing a structured command system, each team understood its responsibilities, reducing redundancy and ensuring that every resource was used to its fullest potential.

For instance, during large-scale emergencies, an updated incident command system allows leaders to dynamically assign roles based on evolving situations and ensures that all members work harmoniously towards a common goal. It empowers decision-makers to efficiently manage human and material resources, reinforcing the department's capacity to handle complex scenarios. This systemic coordination resulted in fewer missed communications and fostered an environment where informed decisions could be made swiftly, even under pressure.

Another critical facet of increasing efficiency has been through advances in training policies. Recognizing the ever-evolving nature of firefighting techniques, Chief Neal introduced revamped training schedules that align with national standards, focusing on modern methods and technologies. These rigorous training programs are designed not only to hone the skills of the firefighters but also to instill a culture of continuous learning and adaptation. By keeping pace with contemporary firefighting strategies, the department ensures its personnel are well-prepared to tackle current challenges effectively.

Training modules now emphasize new tools and techniques, providing hands-on experience in simulated environments. Through these exercises, firefighters gain practical knowledge of advanced equipment and learn to respond adeptly to diverse scenarios. The department also scheduled regular refresher courses, preventing skill deterioration and maintaining high professional standards. Consequently, firefighters can apply innovative solutions in the field, reflecting the department's commitment to being at the forefront of firefighting practices.

Complementing these measures, the creation of comprehensive policy manuals provided the backbone for clear operational guidelines. These manuals became indispensable resources, offering firefighters and administrative staff alike a well-defined framework for action. Each policy manual was crafted to address specific scenarios, guiding personnel through step-by-step procedures required in various high-stress situations. Having these references at hand enabled informed decision-making, reduced ambiguity, and assured consistent application of protocols across all levels of the department.

Comprehensive policy manuals also served as training aides themselves, allowing both new recruits and seasoned veterans to familiarize themselves with expectations and procedures. The clear documentation supported accountability and transparency, reinforcing the importance of adherence to established guidelines. To facilitate their effectiveness, versions of these manuals were updated regularly to integrate feedback and accommodate any changes in best practices or regulations.

Moreover, these manuals laid out the guidelines necessary for navigating intricate scenarios, such as multi-agency collaborations or dealing with hazardous materials incidents. By establishing guidelines on effective communication during organizational changes, they ensured smooth transitions and minimized disruptions. Clear communication channels are essential during shifts in policy, preventing misunderstandings and aligning everyone with newfound directives. Furthermore, defined communication protocols encouraged sharing information freely, ensuring all stakeholders remained informed and prepared to adapt promptly.

Fostering Collaborative Change and Continuous Improvement

Strategic adjustments to policies and procedures within the Balch Springs Fire Department have significantly enhanced efficiency under

Chief Neal's leadership. Central to this transformation is the goal of fostering continuous improvement and adaptability through collaborative change management and thorough evaluation. The first step in this process involved establishing open communication channels that allowed firefighters to share insights and ideas freely. Encouraging this dialogue not only cultivated a sense of ownership among team members but also engaged them deeply in the process of improvement.

Firefighters, who are often on the frontline facing myriad challenges, possess firsthand knowledge that can lead to innovative solutions. By creating an environment where their voices were heard and valued, Chief Neal enabled the department to harness these unique perspectives. This participatory approach empowered team members while simultaneously driving meaningful improvements in service delivery. As firefighters contributed to policy reforms, they became active participants in their own professional development, thereby bolstering morale and building a culture of shared accountability.

Simultaneously, the department embraced new technologies with an emphasis on user-friendly integration. Introducing technological advancements served dual purposes: enhancing the proficiency of teams and raising operational standards. By ensuring that new tools were straightforward and effective, staff could quickly learn and apply them, avoiding disruptions in workflow. For instance, training sessions focused on real-world applications of technology helped bridge any gaps between traditional techniques and modern equipment use. By selecting intuitive systems, the department minimized resistance to change, allowing for smoother transitions and better performance outcomes. This adoption of technology was not merely about keeping pace but about setting new benchmarks in service excellence.

In parallel, systematic performance evaluations were implemented as a key aspect of ongoing development. Ensuring transparency and consistency, these evaluations provided a clear picture of the department's capabilities and areas needing attention. Regular assessments helped identify strengths and deficiencies, offering valuable data to inform strategic decisions. To reinforce credibility, benchmarking against top-performing agencies was adopted. By measuring their performance against the best in the field, the department gained insights into successful practices and standards to aspire toward. Establishing a guideline for implementing these evaluations emphasized the importance of structured review processes in maintaining and improving departmental effectiveness.

Constructive feedback loops were integral to the entire strategy. Regular and comprehensive feedback ensured that all efforts were recognized, and areas needing refinement were addressed promptly. This cycle of feedback encouraged self-reflection and adaptation, enabling the department to remain responsive to changing demands and emerging challenges. Although the guideline for encouraging self-reflection was not strictly necessary, fostering a mindset open to constructive criticism was essential for continuous progress. When personnel felt appreciated and their contributions acknowledged, motivation soared, leading to higher levels of engagement and commitment to the department's objectives.

Ultimately, instilling a culture of continuous refinement anchored the entire approach to process evolution. Fostering an environment where regular assessment and adaptation became second nature required both leadership vision and everyday practice. Through deliberate efforts in communication, technology integration, performance evaluation, and feedback, Chief Neal's changes proved transformative. By aligning operational goals with the evolving needs of the community and leveraging the collective expertise of his team, the foundation was laid for sustained growth and innovation. Implementing a culture of ongoing improvement not only aligned with best practices but also acted as a catalyst for future success, ensuring that efficiency and effectiveness would continually advance to meet future challenges head-on.

This approach made it clear that adaptability was not just a strategy but a core principle guiding every decision. Chief Neal's emphasis on dynamic procedures allowed the fire department not only to respond more effectively to emergencies but to anticipate and prepare for future demands. The combination of open communication, strategic use of technology, rigorous evaluation, and acknowledgement formed an ecosystem within the department that thrived on shared goals and mutual respect.

Through these measures, the Balch Springs Fire Department transformed into a model of efficiency and responsiveness. It stood as a testament to what could be achieved when a team works cohesively towards common aims, guided by leadership committed to progressive change. The department's journey underscored the power of innovation paired with a dedication to community service, illustrating how thoughtful procedural adjustments could lead to remarkable achievements in public safety and service delivery.

Concluding Thoughts

Throughout this chapter, we have examined how Chief Neal's strategic adjustments to policies and procedures have significantly bolstered the efficiency and effectiveness of the Balch Springs Fire Department. The integration of technology such as the computer-Aided Dispatch (CAD) system transformed emergency response dynamics by reducing response times and enhancing communication between dispatchers and responders. This technological advancement has not only streamlined operations but also improved resource allocation through data analytics, making the department more proactive in its approach. By embracing updated incident command systems, the department has established clearer communication and command structures, which have minimized confusion and redundancy during emergencies. Additionally, a focus on modern training techniques has ensured that firefighters are equipped with contemporary skills, enabling them to tackle evolving challenges with confidence.

Alongside operational advancements, fostering collaborative change has been key to continuous improvement within the department. Open communication channels have encouraged firefighters to share insights, sparking innovative solutions and a sense of ownership over the improvements. Embracing user-friendly technologies and conducting systematic performance evaluations have further reinforced operational standards. These efforts have fostered an environment where constructive feedback is valued, driving ongoing refinement and responsiveness to new demands. Ultimately, under Chief Neal's leadership, the department has transformed into a model of efficiency and adaptability, exemplifying the power of thoughtful procedural adjustments paired with a dedication to community service. Through these measures, the department remains prepared to meet future challenges while consistently advancing its mission of public safety and service delivery.

Chapter 19: Reflecting on the First Year

Successes and Setbacks

Reflecting on the first year of Chief Neal's leadership at the Balch Springs Fire Department offers a unique insight into both the achievements and challenges faced during this transformative period. Leading any organization comes with its own set of trials, but within the critical service sector of firefighting, these stakes are particularly high. As members of a community-focused department, the firefighters under Chief Neal were tasked with not only addressing the immediate needs for emergency response but also with adapting to changes in leadership style and operational directives. The inaugural year under new leadership serves as the backdrop for an intricate examination of what progress looks like when viewed through the dual lens of success and obstacle navigation.

The chapter delves into a thorough analysis of how victories were celebrated, and community bonds were strengthened under Chief Neal's guidance. Key initiatives like peer-to-peer recognition programs and innovative community outreach activities played crucial roles in shaping departmental culture and public perception. The narrative highlights specific cases where recognizing contributions, both internally among staff and externally with residents, translated into increased morale and trust. Furthermore, leadership development and mental health support emerged as pillars for sustainable growth, underscoring the importance of holistic approaches to professional and personal well-being. This reflective account provides readers with a balanced view of the strategic efforts that defined Chief Neal's first year, offering lessons and inspiration for driving positive change in similar organizations.

Celebrating Successes & Community Bonds

The first year under Chief Neal's leadership at the Balch Springs Fire Department marked a period of transformation and achievement. At the heart of this success was an emphasis on regularly celebrating both small and large victories. Recognizing achievements is more than just a morale booster; it acts as a potent tool for maintaining motivation and cohesion within the team. Whether it's achieving a departmental objective or overcoming a challenging emergency scenario, each victory contributes to building a strong, united workforce. Celebrations became regular events in the department's calendar, allowing team members to pause, appreciate their hard work, and find renewed energy for future tasks.

To further enhance this culture of acknowledgment, the implementation of peer-to-peer recognition programs played a pivotal role. These programs created an environment where team members not only received recognition from their supervisors but also from their colleagues. This approach fostered a deeper sense of unity and mutual appreciation among firefighters, as it empowered them to acknowledge each other's contributions directly. Peer recognition cultivated respect and camaraderie, reinforcing collective goals over individual accolades. Acknowledging everyday efforts ensured that no act, regardless of its size, went unnoticed, hence strengthening overall morale.

Another cornerstone of Chief Neal's successful year was the development of comprehensive community outreach initiatives. One standout effort was the introduction of fire safety workshops tailored specifically for local residents. These initiatives aimed at not only educating the public about fire safety practices but also enhancing trust and familiarity between the fire department and the community. By engaging with the residents directly, the department broke down barriers and built enduring relationships. Interactive sessions not only equipped individuals with essential safety skills but also personalized the presence of the fire department in people's daily lives. This engagement led to increased community support and a shared commitment to public safety.

In addition to these initiatives, Chief Neal prioritized open communication and transparency as foundational elements of his leadership strategy. Ensuring that the community was well-informed about the department's activities and capabilities helped gain their confidence. Regular updates, whether through public forums, newsletters, or social media, kept the public in the loop regarding departmental progress and challenges. This transparency fostered a culture of accountability and reassured the community of the department's dedication to their safety and well-being. When citizens are knowledgeable about and confident in their fire department, it paves the way for meaningful collaboration and support in times of need.

Leadership Development & Mental Health Support

In Chief Neal's first year with the Balch Springs Fire Department, one of the pivotal initiatives was the launch of mentorship and training programs aimed at nurturing leadership skills among emerging leaders within the department. Recognizing that the strength of an organization fundamentally rests upon its leaders, this initiative focused on equipping promising individuals with the knowledge and skills necessary for effective leadership. The program offered a combination of formal training sessions and hands-on experiences, allowing participants to engage directly with the daily operations and decision-making processes of the department.

The mentorship aspect of the program paired these rising leaders with experienced senior officers who provided guidance, shared insights from their careers, and offered practical advice. This relationship fostered an environment where mentees could safely explore new ideas, make mistakes, and learn from those experiences. As a result, participants gained not only technical expertise but also the confidence and strategic thinking required to act decisively in high-pressure situations—a vital competency in firefighting and emergency response scenarios.

Additionally, active involvement of these budding leaders in decision-making processes was essential. By participating in meetings and operations evaluations, they contributed meaningful insights and suggestions, grounding their academic training in real-world applications. This opportunity to influence departmental policies and procedures not only granted them invaluable experience but also underscored the importance of diverse perspectives in shaping effective strategies and solutions. By tapping into the potential of these individuals, the department not only strengthened its leadership pipeline but also ensured that it was aligned with modern practices conducive to its future success.

Parallel to fostering leadership growth, Chief Neal emphasized improving mental health support within the department. Recognizing the demanding nature of their work, the fire department established a comprehensive mental health support system to safeguard personnel well-being. The system included access to professional counseling services, enabling staff to address and manage stress, trauma, and other mental health challenges associated with their roles.

Peer support groups were another crucial component of this mental health framework. These groups provided a platform for open discussions about personal experiences and coping mechanisms, fostering camaraderie and mutual support among team members. Sharing struggles and successes in a safe space helped normalize conversations about mental health, contributing to a culture where seeking help was viewed as a strength rather than a weakness.

Furthermore, creating an environment that encouraged mental health discussions was an integral part of destigmatizing the subject.

By bringing mental health dialogues into routine meetings and training sessions, Chief Neal and his team worked tirelessly to break down the barriers and misconceptions surrounding mental health care. Open communication was actively promoted, with workshops and seminars aimed at educating personnel about signs of mental distress and available resources.

This multifaceted approach not only addressed existing mental health issues but also proactively equipped team members with the tools needed to maintain their mental resilience. The emphasis on mental well-being echoed throughout the department's daily operations, emphasizing its critical importance alongside physical safety and operational readiness.

Guidelines for encouraging such advancements in mental health support were simple yet impactful: prioritize accessibility to mental health resources, encourage openness by setting examples at the leadership level, and regularly evaluate the effectiveness of implemented measures to ensure they meet the evolving needs of staff. These steps served as foundational elements in establishing a supportive workplace culture where individuals felt both valued and cared for.

Through these strategic initiatives revolving around leadership development and mental health enhancement, Chief Neal set a precedent for holistic growth within the Balch Springs Fire Department. His efforts highlighted the department's commitment not only to operational excellence but also to the personal and professional development of its members. The integration of these programs underscored an understanding that each firefighter's well-being was intrinsically linked to their performance and, ultimately, to the safety and efficacy of the entire department.

Summary and Reflections

Chief Neal's leadership during his inaugural year with the Balch Springs Fire Department exemplifies a profound focus on transformation and growth. By prioritizing celebrations of success, from major achievements to everyday victories, he created an environment that fostered unity and motivation among team members. The empowerment of peer-to-peer recognition further amplified this sense of community, allowing for a culture where acknowledgments were not limited to hierarchical structures. His strategic initiatives extended into the community, forging new bonds through fire safety workshops and transparent communication, which enhanced public trust and confidence in the department. These efforts laid a robust foundation for continued collaboration between the fire department and the residents it serves, making public safety a shared endeavor.

Additionally, Chief Neal championed the personal and professional development of his team, recognizing the pivotal role of leadership and mental health support. Through comprehensive mentorship and training programs, emerging leaders were equipped with essential skills, shaping a forward-thinking department ready to tackle future challenges. Simultaneously, his commitment to mental well-being initiated a paradigm shift, normalizing conversations around mental health and dismantling associated stigmas. This holistic approach underscored the significance of each firefighter's welfare in enhancing both their individual performance and the overall effectiveness of the department. The integration of these multifaceted strategies has set a precedent within the department, highlighting Chief Neal's dedication to operational excellence and a supportive workplace culture that values every member as crucial to its success.

Chapter 20: A Vision for the Future

Year Two and Beyond

Leading the Balch Springs Fire Department into a new era, Chief Neal has been instrumental in transforming its capabilities and operations. His forward-thinking strategy focuses on leveraging advancements to enhance emergency response and improve community safety. This chapter delves into the initiatives that define the fire department's strategic growth under his leadership. From modernizing equipment and facilities to implementing groundbreaking health and safety measures, the department has taken significant steps to ensure readiness for any situation. The goal is not only to meet present challenges but also to anticipate future needs, reflecting a commitment to exceptional service and innovative solutions.

Within these pages, readers will discover the multifaceted approach Chief Neal employs to cultivate resilience and operational excellence. The chapter explores the critical investments made in advanced firefighting technologies and infrastructure improvements, highlighting their impact on efficiency and effectiveness. It also examines the structural changes within the department aimed at fostering leadership and expanding skill sets, with an emphasis on training programs that prepare personnel for diverse emergencies. Additionally, the narrative addresses the department's focus on mental health and community engagement, illustrating how these elements are crucial for a well-rounded public safety strategy. Through this exploration, readers gain insight into how Chief Neal and his team are shaping a future-ready department poised to serve its community with unwavering dedication.

Enhancing Emergency Response Capabilities

Under Chief Neal's visionary leadership, the Balch Springs Fire Department embarked on a transformative journey to enhance emergency response capabilities. This progress was marked by significant advancements in equipment and facilities, all aimed at improving efficiency and ensuring the safety of both personnel and the community they serve.

The department's acquisition of state-of-the-art fire trucks and engines represents its commitment to leveraging technology for better response times and increased operational effectiveness. These vehicles are equipped with cutting-edge tools and systems that allow firefighters to handle emergencies more efficiently. Enhanced navigation systems, advanced water pumps, and thermal imaging cameras are just a few examples of the innovations integrated into these new machines. Such advancements not only streamline operations but also empower firefighters to respond swiftly and accurately to a diverse range of incidents, from structural fires to hazardous material spills.

In line with modernizing its fleet, the department undertook comprehensive renovations of its public safety building. This project was integral in creating an environment that supports the well-being of its personnel. A key component of this upgrade was the implementation of cancer prevention initiatives, addressing one of the most pressing health issues facing firefighters today. The introduction of decontamination zones and specialized cleaning facilities greatly reduces exposure to harmful carcinogens. Additionally, the establishment of gender privacy quarters reflects a progressive approach to fostering an inclusive workplace, acknowledging the diverse needs of its staff and promoting a respectful atmosphere for all members.

Further enhancing operational readiness, the fire department invested in acquiring cutting-edge gear designed to provide maximum protection to its firefighters. New protective clothing and breathing apparatuses incorporate the latest materials and design features to safeguard against the myriad dangers encountered during emergency responses. This sophisticated equipment not only shields firefighters from harm but also contributes to their confidence and morale, knowing they are supported by the best resources available.

Training plays a pivotal role in preparing the department for emergent challenges. Recognizing this, the fire department expanded its training programs to equip personnel with the skills needed to tackle a wide array of situations. Simulation exercises, cross-training opportunities, and collaborative drills were introduced to ensure that every team member is well-versed in handling emergencies ranging from medical crises to natural disasters. This holistic approach to training ensures that firefighters remain adaptable and proficient, fostering a culture of continuous learning and preparedness.

Strengthening Leadership and Personnel Structure

In the progressive transformation of the Balch Springs Fire Department, Chief Neal's vision for restructuring leadership roles has been a pivotal element in fostering accountability and responsibility. At the core of this restructure was the creation of new positions, including an assistant fire chief and lieutenants. These roles were not merely administrative enhancements; they provided crucial opportunities for budding leaders to step forward and demonstrate their capabilities. By expanding the leadership team, the department could delegate responsibilities more effectively, allowing for more granular management and oversight of daily operations. This move also served to streamline decision-making processes and reduce bottlenecks, enhancing overall responsiveness.

This strategic addition of leadership layers didn't happen in isolation. Alongside these new roles, there was a definitive push to attract and retain top talent through competitive salary increases.

Understanding the critical role that competent and dedicated personnel play in public safety, the department opted to enhance its financial incentives. These improvements reflected the department's commitment to acknowledging and rewarding the hard work and expertise of its staff. This approach not only strengthened workforce morale but also positioned the department as a desirable employer within the region, attracting high-caliber professionals who were eager to contribute to public safety.

Further complementing these initiatives was a notable financial investment channeled into personnel development. Recognizing that effective service delivery hinges on well-equipped and well-trained personnel, the department allocated additional resources toward gear acquisition, training programs, and contracted services. While the budgetary adjustments included provisions for modern equipment, it was the emphasis on training that stood out. Personnel were afforded opportunities to upskill and even cross-train across different areas, ensuring versatility and preparedness in handling a spectrum of emergencies. Contracted services also played a role in bringing specialized expertise, supplementing the efforts of internal teams and broadening the department's operational scope.

In support of these structural changes, Chief Neal emphasized collaborative leadership. This approach fostered an environment where open communication channels thrived, enabling team members at all levels to engage with one another constructively. Leadership under Chief Neal encouraged dialogue, where ideas could be freely shared and valued, promoting inclusivity. As a result, there developed a palpable sense of unity and shared purpose among the ranks. Teams were not just working collaboratively but were imbued with a collective spirit aimed at common goals. Engaging each member in discussion and inviting inputs ensured everyone felt a part of the journey, reinforcing a culture of mutual trust and respect.

The restructuring and salary revisions did more than just reshuffle titles or offer financial perks; they were catalysts for wider cultural shifts within the department. By investing in people and prioritizing engagement at all levels, the department laid down a foundation for resilience and innovation. The integration of diverse perspectives from various team members also meant that strategies were more inclusive and grounded in reality, reflecting the actual needs and preferences of those involved in ground-level operations.

Moreover, the focus on leadership development cascaded benefits beyond immediate administrative efficiency. It engendered a generation of leaders who understood the importance of mentorship, peer support, and continuous professional growth. These leaders were encouraged to be proactive and future-oriented, preparing their teams not just for current challenges but for those that lay ahead. The encouragement towards mentorship opened doors for knowledge transfer, ensuring valuable experiences and insights were passed along seamlessly.

The overarching impact of these initiatives is evident in the renewed vigor with which the department operates. Their ability to respond adeptly to incidents, manage community interactions, and fulfill their mandate as protectors of public welfare has seen commendable improvement. It's a testament to how thoughtfully restructured leadership, combined with robust staff development, can enhance functionality and effectiveness in any organization.

Prioritizing Mental Health and Community Engagement

The Balch Springs Fire Department, under the forward-thinking leadership of Chief Neal, has prioritized mental health support and community collaboration as key components of its strategic growth. As first responders navigate daily high-stress situations, the need for a robust mental health program became evident. Recognizing this, the department implemented a comprehensive initiative designed specifically to meet their unique challenges. Through tailored counseling services, stress management workshops, and peer support systems, first responders are equipped with the tools necessary to cope with the emotional demands of their roles. This program not only aims to promote a supportive environment but also actively works towards improving overall staff well-being.

In conjunction with these efforts, encouraging open conversations about mental health has been at the forefront of the department's mission. By fostering an atmosphere where individuals feel safe to express their concerns without judgment, the department seeks to dismantle the stigma often associated with mental health discussions. Regular team meetings and one-on-one check-ins with mental health professionals provide essential platforms for dialogue, allowing personnel to share experiences and advice. This approach nurtures a culture of trust and empathy, crucial elements in any organization striving for excellence and cohesion.

Further enhancing this holistic strategy is the active pursuit of community feedback and engagement. The fire department understands that its vision must align with the needs and concerns of the residents it serves. By holding town hall meetings, conducting surveys, and maintaining open lines of communication with community leaders, the department ensures that it remains attuned to the public's pulse. This two-way dialogue not only informs the department's actions but also fosters a sense of shared responsibility between the department and the community.

Given the emphasis on community involvement, it becomes imperative to offer guidelines to maximize effective engagement. Initiatives such as regular community forums, suggestion boxes placed in easily accessible locations, and online forums for real-time feedback facilitate interaction. Residents are encouraged to voice concerns, share ideas, and participate in shaping the service they receive. These guidelines serve as a roadmap to ensure that community voices are not only heard but also valued and integrated into the department's strategic planning.

At the core of this endeavor is the integration of mental health and community partnership, which underscores a holistic approach to achieving service excellence and building community trust. Such integration is pivotal in redefining the role of a fire department beyond emergency response. It illustrates a commitment to nurturing resilient communities by recognizing that frontline workers' well-being directly impacts their ability to serve effectively. Programs designed to support mental health, paired with active community participation, bridge the gap between the department and its residents, cultivating an environment of mutual respect and cooperation.

This approach has manifested tangible benefits in the department's operations and community relations. Personnel report higher job satisfaction and improved morale due to the support systems in place, leading to increased productivity and engagement in their duties. Similarly, the establishment of strong community ties has bolstered the department's reputation as a transparent and accountable entity committed to serving its populace. Residents, in turn, have expressed greater confidence in their local fire department, knowing that their input shapes policies and initiatives.

Looking ahead, sustaining this momentum requires continuous evaluation and adaptation to emerging trends and challenges. Chief Neal's leadership exemplifies a proactive stance, emphasizing ongoing education and training focused on mental resilience and cultural competence. By investing in these areas, the department not only supports its workforce but also stands prepared to meet the evolving needs of its community.

Bringing It All Together

Under Chief Neal's dynamic leadership, the Balch Springs Fire Department has embarked on a transformative journey to enhance its emergency response capabilities and strengthen its organizational structure. This chapter detailed the department's strategic initiatives across various domains, from modernizing equipment and facilities to implementing health and safety improvements for staff. By acquiring advanced vehicles and protective gear, and upgrading facilities with cancer prevention measures, the department has not only improved its operational readiness but also fostered a positive and supportive work environment. Alongside physical upgrades, expanded training programs have equipped personnel with vital skills, ensuring they remain adaptable and proficient in diverse emergency scenarios.

Chief Neal's commitment to fostering progressive leadership and prioritizing mental health marks a significant shift in departmental culture. The restructuring of roles, along with competitive salary adjustments, has cultivated a sense of empowerment and unity among staff, encouraging a collaborative approach that values each member's contributions. These developments emphasize a holistic growth strategy, inviting community engagement while supporting firefighter well-being. As we look ahead, sustaining these efforts will be crucial in maintaining the momentum and resilience built over these transformative years. Through strategic foresight and effective implementation, the department stands poised to meet current and future challenges, safeguarding both its personnel and the broader community it serves.

Reference List

(2014). Fema.gov. https://emilms.fema.gov/is_0553a/groups/109.html

Automatic and Mutual Aid. (n.d.). Www.ettfire.com. https://www.ettfire.com/automatic_aid.html

Helping Each Other - what is Mutual or Automatic Aid between FD's? (n.d.). Plumas County Fire Chiefs Association. https://www.plumasfirechiefs.org/helping-each-other—-what-is-mutual-or-automatic-aid-between-fds.html[1]

Shoaf, K. I., Kelley, M. M., O'Keefe, K., Arrington, K. D., & Prelip, M. L. (2014, November). *Enhancing Emergency Preparedness and Response Systems: Correlates of Collaboration between Local Health Departments and School Districts.* Public Health Reports. https://doi.org/10.1177/00333549141296s414

---

1. https://www.plumasfirechiefs.org/helping-each-other---what-is-mutual-or-automatic-aid-between-fds.html

About the Author

Eric J. Neal is a Fire Chief and Emergency Management Director with a Master's in Public Administration and a Bachelor's in Emergency Management. He has served in departments across Texas and Tennessee, sharing his expertise through mentorship and education. His first year as Fire Chief inspired this book, offering lessons for leaders in fire service.